MOTHER TERESA

Emma Johnson

FRANKLIN WATTS
LONDON•SYDNEY

Maps Ian Thompson
Designer Steve Prosser
Editor Simon Adams
Art Director Jonathan Hair
Editor-in-Chief John C. Miles
Picture Research Susan Mennell

Consultant Eileen Yeo
Professor of Social and Cultural
History, University of Strathclyde

© 2003 Franklin Watts

First published in 2003
by Franklin Watts
96 Leonard Street
London
EC2A 4XD

Franklin Watts Australia
45-51 Huntley Street
Alexandria
NSW 2015

ISBN 0 7496 4696 9

A CIP catalogue record
for this book is available
from the British Library.

Printed in Hong Kong/China

Picture credits
Front cover: Topham Picturepoint/UPI
(main); Topham/AP(background)
Back cover: Topham Picturepoint/UPI

*Every effort has been made to
contact copyright holders of material
reproduced in this book. Any
omissions will be rectified in
subsequent printings if notice is
given to the publisher.*

Camera Press/Sunil Kumar Dutt
pp.44, 46, 55, 57, 84, 87
Robert Harding Picture Library
pp.12, 15 (Phillip Craven)
Link Picture Library/Dinodia/Sunil
Kumar Dutt pp.50, 52, 58, 65, 66, 90
Magnum Photos p.49 (Raghu Rai),
Popperfoto pp.7, 18-19, 30-31, 32,
35, 43, 78 (Kamal Kishore/Reuters),
89 (Darren Whiteside/Reuters), 92, 95,
96, 99 (Jayanta Shaw/Reuters), 101
(Emmanuel Dunand/AFP)
Public Record Office Image Library
pp.23, 25, 61, 70
Still Pictures pp.73 (Mark Edwards),
74 (Hartmut Schwarzbach)
Topham Picturepoint pp. 2(UPI),
3(UPI), 5(Brian Little/PA), 17, 41(UPI),
43, 62, 69(AP), 70, 77, 81, 82

Mother Teresa 1910–97

Contents

Agnes **6**

The novice nun **14**

Sister Teresa **22**

India before independence **28**

A simple white sari **38**

Scratching letters in the sand **42**

Serving the poor **48**

Sisters of charity **54**

Pure hearts **60**

The homeless of Sealdah Station **68**

The unwanted **72**

The making of a myth **80**

Mother Teresa's way **86**

Mother of the world **94**

Glossary **102**

Further reading **105**

Timeline **106**

Index **110**

Introduction

At the end of the first decade of the 20th century, a baby girl was born in a small Balkan town.

This little girl grew up to be a woman regarded by many as a living saint. By the time of her death, through her actions and example, she had influenced and affected the lives of millions.

In a world increasingly menaced by political and civil strife, disease and wars, many people believed that this woman showed a way – quite outside the corrupt world of politics and the self-interest of multinational companies – to help the poor and the disadvantaged of the world.

Catholic missionaries had long been a presence in India, China, Africa and South America, and it was in India that Mother Teresa would spend her life working for the poor and sick. The life of a missionary was hard. Rarely were there enough resources to deal with the problems that these dedicated people encountered in their work. Often, they were accused of wanting to convert the native population to Christianity above all else, and in some cases this was true.

When Mother Teresa started her missionary work in 1948, India – then as now – was a complex and diverse country, made up of people of many different religions, politics and languages. It had a huge and expanding population and its cities were crammed full of homeless people living on the streets, often right next to large houses occupied by the very rich.

It was in one of these cities – Calcutta, in the north-east of the country – that Mother Teresa worked and died. She dedicated her life to the poor, the sick and the destitute she found on the streets, helping them when no other person or agency would.

▶ *Mother Teresa, photographed in the early 1990s.*

Agnes

On 26 August 1910 a girl was born into a Roman Catholic Albanian family living in the town of Skopje.

Skopje was at that time part of the Turkish Ottoman Empire; from 1912 it was part of the kingdom of Serbia. The girl was the youngest of the three children of Nikola and Drana Bojaxhiu.

When she was one day old the girl was christened Agnes, although her family always called her Gonxha, which means "flower bud". She grew up in a comfortable home with her sister Age and brother Lazar, part of a close and loving family she later described as being "exceptionally happy".

Both of Agnes's parents were caring, public-spirited people. Nikola, known to his friends as "Kole", was a successful businessman and merchant who travelled widely, dealing in medicines and imported goods from Italy. He was also involved in local politics as the only Catholic member of the town council, and was responsible for the building of houses and Skopje's first theatre. The family was devoutly religious and Nikola gave generously to the Catholic church.

He also set an example to the community by giving poor people meals in his own home. Drana often took the children to morning mass. She also taught them to pray and help those people less fortunate than themselves.

All three Bojaxhiu children went to a Catholic church school, where at first lessons were in Albanian and later in Serbo-Croat. Their father encouraged them to work hard at their lessons. Often, he brought back presents from his business trips abroad and entertained them with tales of his many adventures.

The star pupil

As a young child Agnes was often ill and confined to her bed. She suffered from malaria and whooping cough and also had a club-foot. Perhaps partly as a result of her frequent confinement, she became an avid reader, and the knowledge she gained from books during these enforced periods of inactivity helped her to become one of the top students at her school.

▲ This view of Skopje dates from about 1910, the year Agnes was born. It shows the town's impressive multi-arched bridge, which was built by the Romans.

THE BALKANS
as they were in 1914

BOSNIA-HERZEGOVINA

SARAJEVO

SERBIA

BELGRADE

MONTE-NEGRO

Kosovo

ALBANIA

SKOPJE

ITALY

ADRIATIC SEA

ROMANIA

BULGARIA

BLACK SEA

GREECE

AEGEAN SEA

OTTOMAN EMPIRE

Albania

In 1910 – the year of Agnes's birth – Albania was a province within the decaying Ottoman Empire. That same year, Albania first rose in revolt against Ottoman rule. Albanian nationalists, including Agnes's parents, supported those fighting for their freedom and were optimistic that Albania would soon become an independent nation for the first time in its history.

Albania's powerful neighbours – Greece and Serbia – did not support this revolt, since it would make it harder for them to carve up Albania between themselves. Serb hatred of the Albanians was long-standing and in 1912,

when war broke out across the Balkans against Ottoman rule, there were massacres of Albanians in Serbia.

In October 1912 the Serbs occupied Skopje and the outlook looked grim. Then Austria, which supported an independent Albania to counteract Serbia, came to the rescue. Most of Albania was granted independence the next year, athough Skopje and the surrounding area became part of Serbia. The Bojaxhiu family were now in a double minority: they were Albanian and Catholic but found themselves in a country that was Serb and Orthodox Christian.

When Agnes was eight years old her father was taken ill after attending a political dinner in Belgrade, the capital of Serbia. This dinner was one of many meetings being held to discuss regional politics. The borders of some Balkan countries were being redrawn after World War One (1914–18) and most Albanians wanted to add the largely Albanian-populated province of Kosovo – to the north of Skopje and also part of Serbia – to their own country. It is thought that political rivals had poisoned Nikola. Nothing could be done to help him and he died some days later, aged just 45.

Large crowds came to Nikola's funeral and, following the local tradition, handkerchiefs were given to all the children at the funeral to dry their tears as well as to keep in remembrance of him. After her husband's sudden death, Drana Bojaxhiu couldn't keep the family business going and, apart from their home, the family lost everything.

Distraught with grief, Agnes's mother at first let the responsibility for all decisions rest with her oldest child Age, who was 15, but soon she started to think about the future. With three children to support, Drana needed to start a new business. She began producing and selling clothing and fine embroidery, drawing on her needlework skills. Soon she had built a new life for herself and her family.

Setting an example

Although the family was no longer wealthy, Drana continued to help those in need, giving food and assistance to the sick, poor and elderly. The example that both her parents set stayed with Agnes for the rest of her life, teaching her to treat adversity as a challenge and never to give up the struggle to help other people.

The family's religious convictions never wavered either. Drana and her three children prayed together each day and celebrated all the religious festivals. Once a year they made a pilgrimage to the shrine of the Madonna of Letnice in the mountains of Montenegro. They travelled in a horse-drawn carriage. This was their holiday and often they spent a few weeks there in the hope that the fresh air would help Agnes's health.

After primary school, the Bojaxhiu children all went to the state gymnasium

▲ *Agnes Bojaxhiu (right) in 1924 with brother Lazar and sister Age. Shortly after this photograph was taken Lazar left to go to the military academy.*

(secondary school) in Skopje. Agnes appeared to have a real gift for writing. Her older sister Age was also considered to be very bright and went on to study economics at a commercial college. Both girls were members of the church choir and sang in festivals and at charity concerts. A local musician taught Agnes to play the mandolin and found her to be a willing and able pupil.

In 1924 Agnes's brother Lazar won a scholarship – the Sabri Qytezi Prize – and went to Austria for a year to study. On his return he joined the military academy in Tirana, the capital of Albania, later becoming a lieutenant in the Albanian army and then an attendant to King Zog I, the new king of independent Albania.

As teenagers, Agnes and Age took part in many church activities and Agnes became one of the leading members of a society for young Catholic girls. They lived next to the parish church of the Sacred Heart of Jesus; Lazar said that sometimes his mother and sisters spent as much time there as they did at home.

The Catholic society that Agnes attended often organized outings, meetings and lectures and it was here that she first heard of missionary work in India. Local priests who had been sent to convert Indians to Christianity wrote letters home describing their work. These letters captured Agnes's imagination and made her want to follow in their footsteps.

Later in life she said that as a young teenager she had no plans to become a nun, but by the time she was 18 she had decided that it was her calling to be a Christian missionary.

The calling

When Agnes told her mother how she felt, Drana was proud that her daughter wanted to become a nun. Nevertheless, she was concerned about all the things Agnes would have to give up in order to follow her calling. She knew it would be hard for her daughter to be parted from her family forever and to give up any thought of becoming a mother herself. She gave Agnes this advice: "My daughter, if you begin something, begin it with your whole heart. Otherwise, don't begin it at all."

Agnes and her mother also consulted their local priest, a Jesuit named Franjo

▲ A view of Agnes (far left) with schoolfriends in about 1920. She is dressed in black as she is in mourning for her father who died the year before.

What became of Age?

Age, Agnes's older sister, remained with her mother in Skopje until 1932, when she moved to Tirana – the capital of Albania – to live with her brother, Lazar. She became a translator (from Serbo-Croat into Albanian) and later worked for Albanian radio.

The Roman Catholic Church

During the time Agnes was growing up, the pope was Pius XI. The pope is the head of the Roman Catholic Church; his headquarters are at the Vatican in Rome.

Catholicism teaches that God came to redeem the world through his son Jesus Christ. Catholics pray not only to God and Christ but also to Christ's mother, the Blessed Virgin Mary, and to the saints (people who have gained a special place in heaven through holy deeds in life). The hierarchy of the Catholic Church is very complex, but at the lowest level is the parish priest who, for most Catholics, is a central figure in their everyday lives.

Catholic nuns believe they are the "Brides of Christ" and must take vows of poverty, chastity and obedience. This means that they live as a part of an order, or religious community. They have very few personal possessions, do not have relationships with members of the opposite sex and must obey the rules of the order.

Different orders do different kinds of work. Some are cloistered, which means that the nuns live exclusively in a convent and have little contact with the outside world. Members of other orders work as teachers or nurses. Whatever the type of order, prayer and self-sacrifice are integral parts of a nun's life.

◀ A view of St Peter's Basilica, the chief church of the Roman Catholic faith. It is located in the Vatican, Rome.

Jambrekovic, but when Agnes thought that she heard the Virgin Mary telling her to answer God's call, her decision was final.

Lazar was against the idea of Agnes becoming a nun. He felt that she should try to make a career of writing and he wrote to try to persuade her not to leave home. But Agnes was determined and wrote back to her brother, saying: "You think you are important, because you are an officer, serving a king of two million subjects. But I am serving the King of the whole world. Which of us do you think is in the better place?"

The novice nun

Agnes's decision to become a nun was a serious one. It meant that she must renounce all personal ties to the world and dedicate her life to God.

In becoming a nun, Agnes would have to take a vow of obedience. Later in her life it might have been hard for her to keep such a vow, since she was often forced to invent her own rules in order to help those in need.

In September 1928 Agnes started her journey to India via Zagreb, Paris, London and Dublin. Her mother and sister wept on the station platform as the train pulled out of Zagreb carrying Agnes away. At just 18 years old she was leaving her home for the first time, never to see her mother again.

Agnes had been advised that the best way to become a missionary in India was to join the Order of the Sisters of Loreto, since members of their community were already working there. She applied to join the Loreto nuns and was asked to attend an interview in Paris with the mother superior of the order. She travelled from

Mary Ward and the Loreto nuns

The Order of the Sisters of Loreto is the Irish branch of the Institute of the Blessed Virgin Mary, founded in 1609 by Mary Ward, an English Catholic. Mary had gone to France to join a community of the Poor Clares in St-Omer but, aged 24, decided that God meant her to do "some other thing". She returned home to recruit nuns who would work outside the confines of the convent. When the nuns left England to set up and run schools for girls, they met with opposition from the Catholic Church. It was not until 1713, nearly 70 years after her death, that Pope Benedict XIII validated her order on the condition that Mary Ward's name was not mentioned as its founder. In 1822 the institute was given a house outside Dublin, which was renamed Loreto Abbey after a town in Italy. The new Loreto Order flourished in Ireland and in 1841 was asked to set up a foundation for education and nursing in Calcutta, India. By the time Agnes joined the order, Mary Ward had been acknowledged once more; she became a source of inspiration to the novice nuns.

▲ Loreto Abbey, near Dublin in Ireland. Agnes joined the Loreto Order because these were the nuns who worked in Calcutta and Bengal. She spent many weeks here learning English.

▲ *Agnes aged 18 – about the time she left Skopje to travel to Ireland.*

On 1 December 1928 she and her former travelling companion, now named Sister Mary Magdalene, left Ireland and began their long sea voyage to India. They travelled on the steamer *Marchait*, which arrived in Colombo, Ceylon (now Sri Lanka) on 27 December. From here Agnes wrote enthusiastic letters to a church magazine – *Catholic Missions* – back home describing the heat, the people and the city with its lush vegetation.

Agnes's chosen name

Agnes identified with a French nun called Thérèse Martin, the "little flower" who prayed for the success of missionaries. Thérèse Martin had spent her short life – she died of tuberculosis aged 24 – within the walls of her convent doing "ordinary things with extraordinary love". Her goodness in performing lowly tasks inspired Catholics everywhere, and in 1927 she was canonized (made a saint) with the title St Thérèse of Lisieux. Because Agnes chose the Spanish spelling of the name, Teresa, many people thought that she was a follower of the well-known Carmelite nun, St Teresa of Avila. Later in her life, Mother Teresa explained to people that she had taken the name of "'the little one', not the big St Teresa of Avila".

Zagreb with another girl, Betika Kajnc, who also wanted to join the Loreto nuns. Both girls were accepted as novices – beginners – and sent, via London, to Loreto Abbey in Ireland, where they spent several weeks learning English. Agnes had inherited her father's gift for languages and picked up her new language easily.

Agnes now became Sister Teresa. She named herself for St Therese of Lisieux, a French nun who believed in "the little way" of working for God, by joyfully carrying out simple tasks as well as she could.

▲ A view of part of the main street of Colombo, Ceylon (now Sri Lanka) in the late 1920s. This city was the first place that the ship carrying the Loreto novices docked in India. The journey took weeks.

17

Catholic Missions

Father Jambrekovic, Agnes's village priest, had introduced her to many Catholic magazines and newspapers that carried letters and articles from missionaries in India and other parts of the world. He also organized collections to support the work of missionaries.

The magazine *Catholic Missions*, published by the Association for the Propagation of the Faith, was a particularly strong influence on young Agnes. During her life in India, she often wrote letters to the magazine. These inspired readers in the same way that the missionaries' letters had inspired her.

The nuns' next stop was the Indian city of Madras, where they walked in the streets and were shocked by the poverty of the people living there. Sister Teresa was horrified to see almost naked people, "wearing at best a ragged loincloth", whose only shelter and bedding were banana leaves. She thought that if Europeans could see this poverty, they would stop grumbling about their own misfortunes and offer up thanks to God for their blessed lives.

The *Marchait* docked in Calcutta on 6 January 1929 and after a week the sisters

▶ *The town of Darjeeling, where Sister Teresa was posted after a week in Calcutta.*

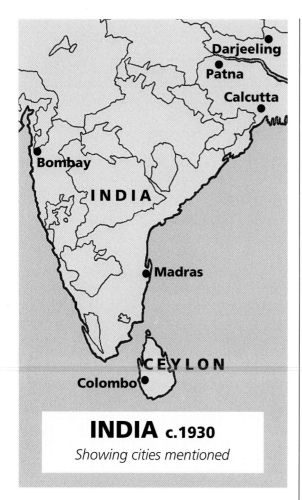

INDIA c.1930
Showing cities mentioned

famous for its tea plantations, but it was also a town set up for leisure, with luxurious hotels and large houses sited to enjoy the cooling breezes and the wonderful views over the hills. In this beautiful setting the young Sister Teresa completed her noviciate, studying theology and the scriptures and learning the local Hindi and Bengali languages while improving her grasp of English.

"Wonderful medicine"

For two hours each morning the novice nuns taught in the Loreto convent school and took turns nursing in a small hospital there. Sister Teresa saw the horrible ulcers, sores and other infections that blighted the lives of the poorest people. She would tell them to bring their children – who could not be cured by their village doctors – to her because she had "wonderful medicine" for them.

These poor people did as she asked and, in her own words, she gave them "holy baptism, eternal blessedness." To Sister Teresa they were getting "the best medicine of all". This religious life suited Sister Teresa very well. From an early age she had an unquestioning

were sent north to Darjeeling in the foothills of the Himalayas. The novice nuns then spent the next two years learning how to live within the rules and traditions of their order.

In 1929 Darjeeling was the town in which wealthy members of the British Raj (government) spent the hot summer months. The area around Darjeeling was

▲ Sister Teresa (left) and another novice pose for a
photograph in 1929.

acceptance of authority, especially within
the Catholic church.

Three months before her 21st birthday
she took her first vows of poverty, chastity
and obedience. The ceremony took place
in Darjeeling on 24 May 1931 and
consisted of the nun lying prone on the
floor in an attitude symbolic of death.
This meant that the sister was leaving all
worldly things behind and that there
would be no going back to her life as it
had been lived before.

Sister Teresa

Soon after taking her first vows, Sister Teresa was sent to Calcutta to start teaching.

Sister Teresa was assigned to the Loreto school in the Entally district of east Calcutta, an industrial area full of factory buildings and slum dwellings. Although the Entally establishment was one of the least prestigious of the Loreto schools, it was like a jewel compared to the other buildings in the area. The convent and its well-kept buildings stood in a large compound of beautiful gardens surrounded by a high solid wall with an impressive entrance framed with classical columns.

About 500 wealthy fee-paying students attended the Entally school, Bengali girls from wealthy Hindu, Parsee and Anglo-Indian backgrounds. Most boarded at the school, where they were taught in English, the language of the rulers of India. But there was also another establishment in the compound called St Mary's, and it was here that Sister Teresa was assigned to teach geography and history. This school educated pupils from middle-class and poorer backgrounds, many of whom were orphans. These children did not pay fees and were taught their lessons in the Bengali language. The educators at St Mary's were mostly Indian women who were members of the Daughters of

Bengal

The province of Bengal, in the north-east of India, is prone to heavy rainfall. Floods often devastate whole districts, destroying crops and leaving many people without homes. Bengal has had a turbulent political and religious history. Conquered by the British in 1757, it was divided into East and West Bengal in 1905.

When India became independent in 1947, East Bengal became East Pakistan, a Muslim province physically separated from the rest of Pakistan by India. Following a civil war in 1971, East Pakistan became the independent Muslim state of Bangladesh, which means "Bengal Nation". West Bengal, where Calcutta is situated, is mostly Hindu. Bengali is spoken in both regions.

▲ *The Entally district of Calcutta, where Sister Teresa started teaching, was filled with crowded streets and* *run-down buildings, as shown in this photo from the 1940s.*

St Anne, a diocesan group. They wore saris instead of nuns' habits and did most of the day-to-day teaching.

A sheltered environment

Sister Teresa spent the next 17 years of her life in this environment. She enjoyed her work and was a good teacher who inspired her students to learn. The nuns were not allowed to leave the shelter of the convent walls except for hospital visits and the once yearly retreat – a sort of holiday – to Darjeeling. Here the nuns would have time for prayer and contemplation before going back to work in their communities.

It was almost impossible for the nuns at Entally to find out what was going on outside, in the real world. It was a time of great change in India, with protests led by Mohandas (Mahatma) Gandhi, India's great leader of the people, against British rule. The nuns in the convent knew little of these events and were protected from news of any kind, including, later on, World War Two. Even when they did leave the convent, they were taken to their destination in a private car, accompanied by another nun. They rarely came into contact with anyone outside their order.

The peaceful, secluded atmosphere of the convent was in sharp contrast to life outside its walls, where the streets were teeming with beggars, the poor and the dying. In 1935, however, Sister Teresa was asked to teach at the school of St Teresa, a short walk from the convent compound. Although it was unusual, she

Calcutta

The city of Calcutta had evolved from a village built on swampy marshland. It was hard to drain and home to mosquitoes and other insects that spread disease. Calcutta, which grew to become the second city in the British Empire after London, was chosen for its trading potential as a port. The city had gained a reputation for greed and vice, but it also boasted fine palaces and wide, gracious streets.

Until 1912 Calcutta was the seat of government for the British Raj. Not far from the grand government buildings, clubs, stores and hotels was the squalor of the back streets, the stinking slums where its lepers and beggars lived. The writer Rumer Godden, who lived in the city in the 1920s and 30s, wrote that, "What was horrifying then was that no one did anything about it." Mother Teresa was to change that.

▲ Calcutta has always been a city of extreme
contrasts. Grand buildings constructed under the
British Raj sit side-by-side with the most appalling
poverty and degradation.

▲ *Sister Teresa (far right, back row) poses with other Loreto nuns after taking her final vows in May 1937.*

was occasionally allowed to walk to this school. Her route took her through the Motijhil slum area, so she was one of a very few nuns who saw the poverty of the slums, or bustees, at first hand. Motijhil means "pearl lake", but in this case the pearl lake was nothing but a pool of discoloured filthy water in the centre of the spreading slum. Hovels constructed from a mixture of mud brick, wood, corrugated iron, old cans and palm thatch sheltered a large number of

desperate people. The awful conditions they had to endure was something that Sister Teresa never forgot.

Many of the older girls at St Mary's belonged to a study group very similar to the one that had influenced the teenage Agnes back in Skopje. These girls often discussed the responsibilities of those with material wealth to those who had less. Sister Teresa encouraged these girls to do what they could for the less fortunate people around them. Many of the girls went on to visit the poor and sick and try to relieve what hardships they could in Motijhil. However, Sister Teresa could not help them in these tasks since the rules of enclosure of the Loreto Order made it impossible for her to leave the convent whenever she wanted to.

Dedicated to God

Sister Teresa took her final vows on 14 May 1937 during a stay in Darjeeling. At the ceremony she repeated the first vows she had taken and became a professed nun dedicated to God for the rest of her life.

Soon after her return to Entally she became the headmistress of St Mary's school. Perhaps life was not as adventurous and exciting as she had thought it might be when, as a teenager in Skopje, she had dreamed of being a missionary in India. She had met no wild animals, nor struggled to find her next meal. Nonetheless, she found herself surrounded by appalling poverty and disease and it would not be long before she discovered her true vocation.

India before independence

In the 18th century the British East India Company and the French East India Company (both founded during the previous century) were in competition with each other for the immense wealth that India possessed. Both countries set up trading posts at Madras, Bombay and Calcutta.

At that time the French and British were at war with one another in Europe and this conflict spilled over into India. The British East India Company became so powerful that it established its own army which, under the command of Robert Clive, defeated the ruler of Bengal at the Battle of Plassey in 1757 and the French in southern India in 1761. After this the British government took an increasing interest in India, taking it over bit by bit using the company's army.

British rule

By the middle of the 19th century, the British East India Company controlled about two-thirds of India. But in 1857–58 a mutiny of Indian troops took place. Although the revolt was crushed, the British government was alarmed enough to take control of India away from the East India Company and govern the country directly.

In 1876 Queen Victoria of Britain was created empress of India and the country became known as "the jewel in the crown" of the British Empire. Under British imperial rule, an Indian middle class began to emerge. Leading members of this class began to push for reforms, leading to the setting up in 1885 of the Indian National Congress, the first step on the road to independence from British rule.

In 1905 the state of Bengal was divided into East and West Bengal.

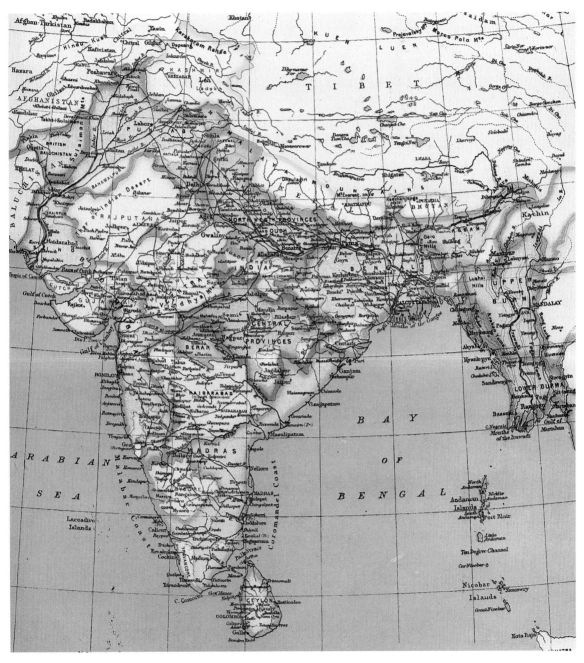

▲ This map from the early 1900s shows the extent of India as a part of the British Empire. Each political division or province was either controlled directly by Britain or by a friendly native (Indian) ruler.

29

This division fragmented the routes of supply and demand from the port of Calcutta to its hinterland. Rivalries soon sprang up between Muslims and Hindus, who had previously co-existed peacefully in the city.

Ending British rule

After a massacre at Amritsar in 1919, when British troops opened fire on an unarmed crowd that had assembled to listen to nationalist leaders, Mohandas Gandhi emerged as the leader of the Indian National Congress.

During the next two decades Gandhi led a movement of civil disobedience and non-cooperation against British rule. Although the British had been the major power in India for more than 150 years, the effect of Gandhi's campaigns was to weaken their control over India. In the years leading up to 1947, when India finally gained its independence, tumultuous events reshaped the country.

Throughout this period, peace and calm reigned within the convent walls

▶ *This 1930s photograph shows the Chowringhee area of Calcutta, where wealthy British and Indians built grand palaces in the 1700s and 1800s.*

▲ *Mohandas Gandhi (centre) leads the Salt March in March 1930 as a protest against unfair British taxes.*

Gandhi's march to the sea

In March 1930, a little over a year after Sister Teresa arrived in India, Mohandas Gandhi led a 480-km march in protest at the British government's Salt Tax, a law designed to limit the production of salt.

Salt was a necessity and this unjust tax raised the price so much that the poor could barely afford to buy it. At dawn on 12 March, Gandhi and a group of protestors set off for the coast north of Bombay. Less than a month later, on 6 April, Gandhi reached the coast. After taking a ceremonial dip in the sea, he risked being arrested for defying the Salt Tax by picking up a small grain of natural sea salt and holding it in his hand. The police were called out to disperse the crowds.

Gandhi's symbolic gesture did not lead to his immediate arrest, but on 5 May, under new laws governing civil disobedience, he was arrested and taken to jail in Bombay. His arrest sparked strikes and rioting across India. At the government-owned salt works at Dharasana, armed police attacked 2,000 Gandhi supporters, injuring many. These actions backfired on the British government when public opinion around the world supported Gandhi and his peaceful protest.

of Entally. The nuns knew almost nothing about the misery and squalor that surrounded them on the streets of the city, and even less of the rioting and bloodshed that affected the country as a whole. In fact they knew almost nothing of events in the world at large.

World War Two

At the outbreak of war in September 1939, Britain's resources were stretched to the limit and few Indians wanted to play any part in their ruler's battles.

One Indian leader, Subhas Chandra Bose, tried to organize an Indian National Army and even declared war on the British in 1943. When the island fortress of Singapore fell to the Japanese in 1942, a stream of defeated soldiers and refugees flooded into India via Burma, putting a further strain on the country's resources. The Japanese, who had airfields in neighbouring Burma, frequently bombed Calcutta and smoke hung in a pall over the city.

Sister Teresa carried on teaching at Entally until 1942, when the entire

Loreto complex – convent, schools and gardens – was taken over by the British army for use as a military hospital. The pupils were moved to hostels a long way from the convent. Sister Teresa took charge of the relocation while continuing to teach at another of the mission's Calcutta schools in Convent Road.

In 1943 famine broke out in Bengal. This followed several years of poor rice harvests and a cyclone, which had destroyed the paddy fields in the winter of 1942. With the Japanese occupying Burma, the rice grown there could no longer be imported to India. It is estimated that around five million people – out of a total Bengali population of 60 million – died of starvation during this shortage.

Unity or partition?

More disaster struck after the end of the war in 1945. Britain was almost on its knees and the newly elected British Labour government decided to give India its independence. Muslim politicians led by Muhammad Ali Jinnah wanted to divide India along religious lines, with a Pakistan for the

Muslims and a Hindustan for the Hindus, but the mainly Hindu-led Indian National Congress was opposed to partition and wanted to keep the country united and secular, that is, non-religious.

Negotiations between the two groups broke down and on 16 August 1946 demonstrations and fierce street fighting erupted in Calcutta. After nine days of rioting, at least 5,000 people were killed while many thousands were injured. Supplies to the school had stopped and Sister Teresa was forced to leave the convent and search for food for the 300 pupils in her charge. Helped by some soldiers, she managed to bring back a large quantity of rice. However, the sights she had seen and the killing she had witnessed on the streets stayed with her forever. That day – Friday 16 August 1946 – came to be known as the "Day of the Great Killing".

In 1947 the British government decided that the only solution was to accept partition of the country. In

▶ *The partition of India in 1947 affected millions. Here, Muslim refugees queue to fill water containers before being transported to safety in Pakistan.*

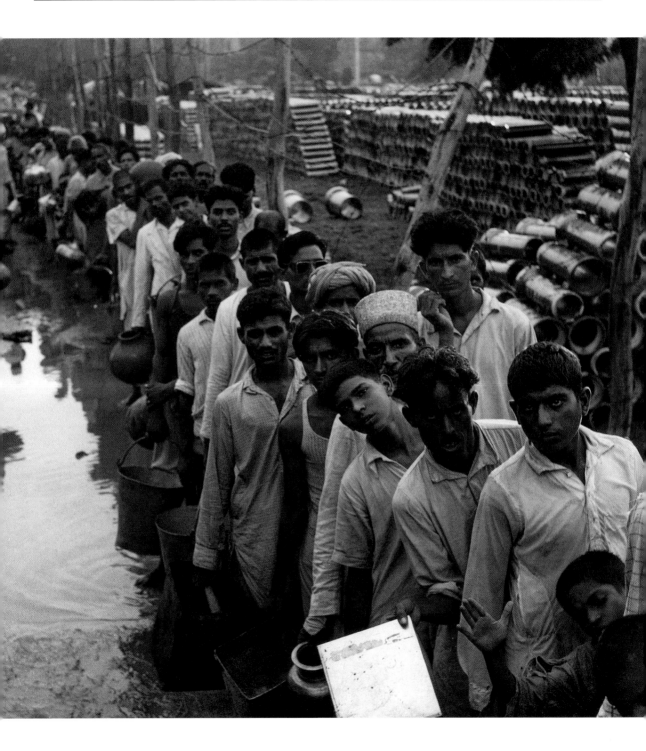

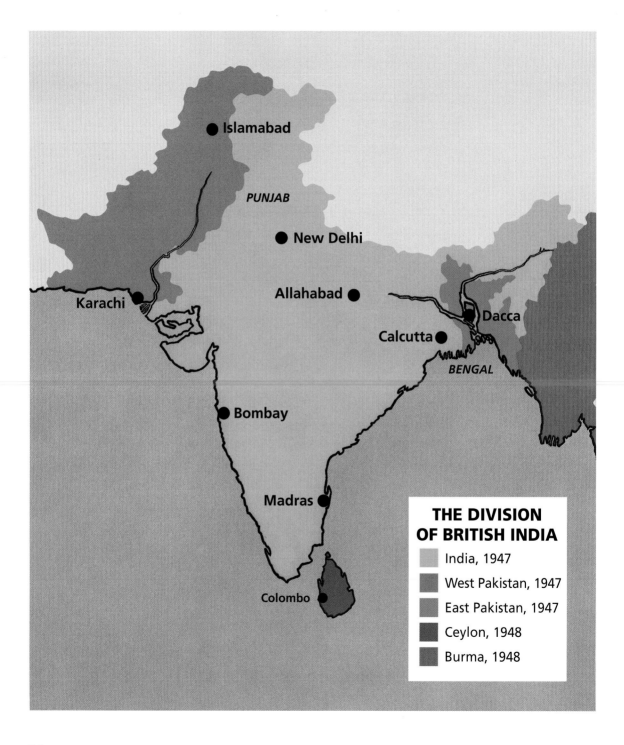

**THE DIVISION
OF BRITISH INDIA**

- India, 1947
- West Pakistan, 1947
- East Pakistan, 1947
- Ceylon, 1948
- Burma, 1948

August a largely Hindu and Sikh India gained its independence alongside the two-part Muslim state of Pakistan.

Further unrest and bloodshed followed in the days and months after independence. East and West Bengal were now part of two separate countries, and huge numbers of Hindus, Sikhs and Muslims found themselves on the wrong side of the new borders. Many were forced to pack what little they could carry and flee – Hindus and Sikhs to India, while Muslims had to choose either East or West Pakistan.

What resulted was one of the largest shifts of population in history, as 16 million people were displaced and entire communities literally torn apart. Such intense disruption had a ripple effect, with violence spreading to most areas of the Indian subcontinent.

Jawaharlal Nehru, one of the leaders of the Indian National Congress, became India's first prime minister and, although there followed a steady growth in industry and agriculture, the substantial increase in population kept the standard of living low for the masses.

A simple white sari

Shortly after witnessing the rioting and killing on the streets of Calcutta, Sister Teresa left the devastated city to go on her annual retreat to the hill town of Darjeeling.

During the train journey, she had plenty of time to examine her thoughts about recent events in the city as well as her experiences in the slums surrounding the Entally compound. She was just 36 years old and was in a mood to review her life so far. She thought about whether she had done what she set out to do in her vocation, and wondered if she could achieve more if she changed her life. She was aware that while she remained within the convent, she was in no position to help the poor in any practical way.

A further call

It was while she was on the train that Sister Teresa experienced what she later referred to as her "call within a call". She was convinced she heard the voice of God telling her that he wanted her to do something different. Later, she told Father Julian Henry, her spiritual director, that

"He was calling me. The message was clear. I must leave the convent to help the poor by living among them." The date of her "call within a call" was 10 September 1946. From that day to this, it is celebrated by the sisters of Mother Teresa's order and referred to as Inspiration Day.

When she returned to Calcutta, Sister Teresa spoke to another priest, Father Celeste Van Exem, who was sympathetic and told her she could do one of two things. She could either write directly to the pope in Rome, asking for a release from the Loreto Order, or he would speak to Archbishop Perier of Calcutta on her behalf and ask him to help. When the archbishop was told of Sister Teresa's plans he was not happy. He didn't like the idea of a nun wandering the streets of a dangerous city like Calcutta. However, he gave her a year to meditate on the idea, hoping that she would change her mind.

Soon after this Sister Teresa was sent to a convent 200 km (130 miles) away in the mining town of Asanol, where she was put in charge of the kitchens and garden. She continued to teach the children at the convent, too, as she waited patiently for the year to go by.

In February 1948 she wrote the pope a letter, the wording of which had been agreed by the archbishop after much discussion. In this letter she asked that she be allowed to return to the secular world and, if her request was granted, no longer to be a nun. She wanted to remain in holy orders but the archbishop would not agree to this. Allowing a nun to break the rules of her order could have had serious effects on church discipline.

A request granted

The archbishop sent Teresa's letter to Delhi, the Indian capital, for forwarding to Rome, but it never reached the Vatican. Church officials in Delhi, aware of the shocking situation in the slums of Calcutta, agreed to her original request. In July 1948 Sister Teresa was given a one-year decree of exclaustration. This meant that she would not have to renounce her vows but could work outside the convent walls for one year to prove that her plans to help the poor were practical.

Teresa had been a sister of Loreto for 17 years and now found it very hard to leave the security of the order. Aged almost 38, excited but full of trepidation, she was about to start the work for which she would become famous throughout the world. She bought a thin white cotton sari with borders edged in blue stripes, a small black crucifix and a rosary. The sari was similar to those worn by the Bengali women who taught at St Mary's school in the Loreto compound. Sister Teresa wore this dress pinned at the left shoulder with the crucifix, her head covered by a cloth of the same design. This clothing set the style of habit for Sister Teresa's followers.

It was arranged that Teresa should spend some time with the Medical Mission Sisters at Patna, 380 km (240 miles) away from Calcutta, before embarking on her new life. The aim was for her to learn as much as possible about nursing and caring for the poor. On 16 August 1948 she quietly left the Entally convent for good and headed for the Holy Family hospital at Patna on the banks of the River Ganges. The medical staff at the hospital were mainly American and European women doctors who specialized in obstetrics and surgery. There were also nurses, laboratory technicians and nutritionists at the centre. The staff ran a school for training nurses and some of these students had attended Loreto schools.

Practical advice

It was when she arrived at Patna that Sister Teresa's strict code of conduct showed itself. She felt strongly that praying at regular hours, fasting and penance were good for the soul. She told some of her co-workers that she wanted to eat only rice and salt, so that she would be even worse off than the poor she was there to help. Worried medical staff explained to her that without regular balanced meals and rest she would not be able to work efficiently in her fight against the effects of poverty. Sister Teresa took this advice on board and remembered it later, when she made sure that her helpers ate a proper breakfast of flat bread chapattis before they went out to work.

Although Sister Teresa already had some nursing experience, she learned at the hospital how to give medicines and injections and deliver babies. She also nursed people who were injured or dying as well as patients infected with diseases such as cholera and smallpox. One of the duties of the nursing sisters was to look after sick children who had been abandoned by parents too poor to afford their medical treatment.

In December 1948 Sister Teresa returned to Calcutta, but before she left the Patna mission, the sisters gave her a truly practical present – a pair of tough sandals. These lasted for many years and were repaired time and time again. In Calcutta she stayed for a few days with the Little Sisters of the Poor, an organization of nuns who ran a home – St Joseph's – for the impoverished elderly. Here she helped to look after the 200 inmates, her final training before starting on her new mission in the Calcutta slums.

The greatest sacrifice

"It was the most difficult thing I have ever done, it was a greater sacrifice than to leave my family and country to enter religious life."
Teresa describes starting her work in the slums of Calcutta.

▶ *This picture of Sister Teresa shows the habit adopted by her in 1948 – a simple blue-edged sari pinned at the left shoulder with a crucifix.*

Scratching letters in the sand

The slums of Calcutta are among the worst in the world. These areas, packed with the poor and dispossessed, exist side by side with well-maintained, prosperous neighbourhoods.

Sister Teresa had seen awful sights in these slums: unwanted babies thrown onto rubbish tips where children searched for something to eat, and people on the streets, too sick to move, being eaten by insects and rats. The luckiest of these people managed to construct shelters with old sacks, but some had no shelter at all and were dressed only in rags.

Into the slums

On 21 December 1948 Sister Teresa began her work. She walked for an hour across the city carrying only a bag containing a small amount of food. She had decided to start her work at Motijhil, the slum she knew best, which was next to her old school of St Mary's inside the Loreto compound. Father Julian Henry, the local priest in Motijhil and Sister Teresa's spiritual director, had often taken girls from St Mary's to work with him among the people in this slum. He had helped and supported Sister Teresa when she decided that her place was among the poorest of the poor.

At first Sister Teresa taught in a run-down courtyard, where her first class consisted of a group of ragged children. She had no chairs and desks, and no books or blackboard, so she asked a man who owned a spade to clear the clumps of grass from the ground. On the newly cleared space she wrote the letters of the Bengali alphabet in the dust with a long stick. Then she taught the children the importance of cleanliness and about the Christian God. By the beginning of January she had three teachers helping

▶ *Calcutta's slums are full of homeless people – such as these boys – who live on the platforms of Howrah railway station.*

42

▲ A homeless orphan, wrapped in a filthy blanket, begs coins from passers-by. It was to help children such as this that Sister Teresa began her mission to educate and care for the poor.

her and more than 50 pupils. On 14 January the schoolroom was ready and when Father Nicaise came to bless it, the children sang a Bengali hymn which Sister Teresa had taught them.

When she started on her new mission, Sister Teresa slept at St Joseph's, about an hour's walk from the slums of Motijhil. This was not a satisfactory arrangement, however, and she began to look for somewhere in Motijhil where she could live and work. It was hard to find a suitable building, so at first she lived in a small hut.

Her first school

The rent for the hut was five rupees (a few pence) a month, which was all Sister Teresa had in her possession at the time. The school was very popular and the number of pupils grew steadily. Then her old friend, Father Van Exem, came to the rescue. He made enquiries on her behalf and found that Michael Gomes, a Roman Catholic Indian, had some space in his house near the slum area.

Gomes's house was a large three-storey colonial building at 14 Creek Lane. It had once been a rather grand place, but now it was run down. Gomes offered

The slum sister

A short time after she started working in Motijhil, Sister Teresa heard rumblings of doubt about her activities there. The local clergy were uncomfortable with a single nun working outside the convent on a mission of her own. They argued that she was a good teacher and her skills were being wasted on the poor. Sister Teresa's response was to say: "If the rich people can have the full service and devotion of so many nuns and priests, surely the poorest of the poor and the lowest of the low can have the love and devotion of us few." Some Indians were also suspicious of the white woman in the sari, accusing her of wanting to convert Hindus to Christianity. She had an answer to this too: *"Ami Bharater Bharat Amar"*, which means "I am Indian and India is mine."

Sister Teresa a large room on the second floor and told her that she could have free use of it as he wanted no rent or food in exchange.

In February 1949 Sister Teresa moved into Creek Lane, bringing with her one chair, a packing case for use as a desk and some other wooden boxes to serve as seats for guests. Now at last she had a base for her work.

▲ A later photograph of Sister (now Mother) Teresa among Indian students at her school. Her pupils were given an education that included practical skills, such as typing, that could be used to earn a living.

Teresa's first full-time helper was Charur Ma, a widow who had been the cook at St Mary's. Soon some of her former pupils at St Mary's heard about her work in Motijhil and came to offer their help too. Others who heard about the new school gave small donations, gifts and equipment. Now, her greatest concern was to obtain medicines to treat the sick who lived on the streets all around her.

Sister Teresa's diary

Archbishop Perier asked Sister Teresa to keep a diary of her year working among the poor of Calcutta. In it she wrote: "God wants me to be a lonely nun." By this she meant that the only way for her to understand the suffering of the poor was to live among them. Prior to this, she had lived a fairly sheltered life, surrounded by people who appreciated and cared for her. Now she was on her own, surrounded by strangers, sometimes forced to beg for provisions. It was a difficult adjustment but it did not weaken her resolve.

Although excerpts from the diary have since been quoted – "Today I learned a good lesson. When I was going until my legs and arms were paining, I was thinking how the poor have to suffer to get food and shelter." – the diary itself has disappeared. Father Van Exem was in possession of it for many years until Teresa asked him to return it. By this time she had achieved widespread public recognition. She may have destroyed the diary, thinking that it exposed too many weaknesses of a time when she was lonely and vulnerable.

Serving the poor

The Gomes family were a great help to Sister Teresa. Because she was a nun she wasn't allowed to go out on the streets alone, so Michael Gomes or his eight-year-old daughter would sometimes accompany her on her errands.

Getting medical supplies for the sick was essential but Sister Teresa often encountered difficulties in obtaining them. On one occasion, when she went to a pharmacy to ask for medicines, the pharmacist refused to help her. She and Gomes sat down patiently to wait in the shop and she quietly recited her rosary. At the end of the day the pharmacist relented and gave her all the things on her list with his firm's compliments.

The first sisters

On 19 March 1949, a month after moving into 14 Creek Lane, the first of the girls who had been her students at St Mary's joined her. Two months later two more followed. The first of these helpers was Subhasini Das, daughter of a well-to-do Bengali family. She had been a boarder at St Mary's from the age of nine and was greatly influenced by her ex-teacher. Later, she took the name Sister Agnes as an acknowledgment of her respect and admiration for Sister Teresa, becoming the first sister of the

▲ *Sister Agnes, who became Sister Teresa's first assistant.*

order founded by her. The other girls took the names of Sister Gertrude and Sister Dorothy.

Soon after returning from the hospital at Patna, Sister Teresa had visited these girls to ask them to join her and to persuade their parents to allow them to do so. The girls' families were not pleased to see their daughters embarking on such unusual work. Going into city slums to help the poor before they had finished their final exams was not acceptable to most wealthy Bengalis. In at least one case, family ties were temporarily severed between parents and daughter, so strong were their feelings about the work Sister Teresa was proposing.

However, Sister Teresa felt a great responsibility towards the girls and found time to coach her ex-students through their final exams. Later, she supported Sister Gertrude in her medical studies, helping her to became the mission's first doctor. Sister Gertrude eventually went to Yemen, where she set up a medical mission for the poor there.

Gradually more recruits arrived to help at the school. By November 1949

▲ Michael Gomes, who provided space for Sister Teresa's school and much other practical help.

Sister Teresa had five helpers. By the start of 1950 there were seven. As the number of followers grew, so too did their need for space. Michael Gomes gave them a larger room and then the loft in his house, still free of charge.

As time went on, extra bathrooms were built with bricks and bamboo matting. Gomes believed that Sister Teresa's presence in his house was a blessing. He could hear the nuns'

▲ *Out among the people. This photograph shows Sister Teresa at work in the slums of Calcutta –* *looking after the destitute and dying, taking in abandoned babies and helping to feed the hungry.*

laughter all over the house and when they were not praying or looking after the poor and sick they sometimes played games such as hopscotch or tug-of-war. After all, in spite of the seriousness of their work, they were still young girls.

Teresa and her first helpers started to gain confidence and soon they were using buses and trams to get around the city to do their work. They spent much of their time trying to help the destitute as well as taking in orphaned or abandoned babies, in addition to any young children who turned up at the refuge each day. One room in Motijhil served as the school, the other as the first refuge for sick and dying destitutes.

Asking for food

Sister Teresa was committed to her "little way", which sometimes meant doing things on a small scale. One of her methods for raising food for the poor and hungry was to go from door to door asking people not to throw away food. She and the sisters would then collect any leftovers to give to those in need. On other occasions she

Early publicity

It was during the first year of her work that Sister Teresa experienced publicity for the first time. A reporter working for a Calcutta-based magazine met her and her helpers and was impressed by the work they were doing. The journalist was Desmond Doig, an Indian Christian of Anglo-Irish extraction who was born in India. After serving with the Gurkhas (Nepalese Hindu soldiers in the British army) during World War Two, he began his journalism career as an illustrator, later becoming a roving reporter who covered stories of general interest around the city.

Doig wrote about Sister Teresa at the start of her mission after being tipped off by a fellow Catholic journalist. This reporter had told Doig to, "Watch this woman, she's quite extraordinary. She's going to be a saint." Later, his own news magazine, the *Junior Statesman*, carried regular articles about Mother Teresa. These were read all over India and influenced a generation of young people who were devoted readers of the magazine.

managed to obtain flour from the government stores. On the way back to Creek Lane, she perched on top of the sacks in the truck to make sure the

flour was not stolen. Sometimes she would leave the house at eight in the morning and not return until five the following morning. She was still working these long hours even when she was in her seventies.

Sister Teresa never seemed to worry about the lack of money – she told the sisters that help would come when it was needed. Her approach to any project seemed to be that no planning or research was necessary because they were doing God's work.

All through their first year, the small group of nuns worked tirelessly to help the poor, sick and dying people around them. If it had not been for their overwhelming faith in their mission, they might have felt crushed by the enormity of their task. As their small community began to grow and their work in the slums of Calcutta became established, they felt they must surely be recognized by the church and granted their own order.

◄ *Sister Teresa's medical training in Patna (p 39) became very useful to her in her work with the sick. Here she supervises the administration of a drip to a patient.*

Sisters of charity

At the end of 1949 Sister Teresa applied for and obtained Indian citizenship. At the end of her trial year of working outside the convent, she drafted the aims and rules of the order she hoped to found.

The most forthright statement in these draft rules was the one which outlined the true purpose of her proposed order: "Our special task will be to proclaim Jesus Christ to all peoples, above all to those in our care." The name she wanted for her organization was the Missionaries of Charity. This also made the evangelical aspect of her movement clear by the use of the word "missionary" in the title. In addition to the familiar vows of poverty, chastity and obedience, a fourth vow was added: "To give wholehearted and free service to the poorest of the poor."

Archbishop Perier was impressed by this document and forwarded it to Rome so that the order could be recognized and approved by the pope. In a remarkably short period of time Pope Pius XII approved the founding of the Order of the Missionaries of Charity. On 7 October 1950 Sister Teresa became Mother Teresa, the founder and head of her own order. The sisters of the Missionaries of Charity wore the same distinctive habit – a white sari with blue borders and a small

A day in the life

The sisters' day followed a strict routine. The morning started at 5 a.m. with prayers, then mass and a sermon at 5.45. After breakfast and chores (cleaning their clothes and rooms), the sisters were engaged in their work with the poor and destitute from 8 a.m. until 12.30 p.m. Lunch was followed by a short rest, after which the sisters were allowed some relaxation, a time when they could read religious books and meditate. The adoration of the Blessed Sacrament took place between 3.15 and 4.30 p.m., followed by an afternoon service for the poor, which lasted until 7.30 p.m. After supper, the day ended with evening prayers at 9 p.m. and bed at 9.45 p.m.

▲ Despite the demands of her work, Mother Teresa made prayer an integral part of each day. This photograph shows her praying with members of her order in Calcutta.

crucifix pinning the cloth on the left shoulder – which Mother Teresa had adopted at the start of her mission. Each sister had just a few possessions: two saris, a pair of sandals, a crucifix, a mattress, a bucket in which to wash themselves and their clothing, and a prayer book.

The expanding order

Over the next two years the number of nuns working within the order grew to almost 30. The house on Creek Lane, which had once seemed so large, could no longer contain them all. It became clear that new premises would have to be found so that the order could continue to help as many needy people as possible.

Father Henry cycled around Calcutta trying to find a larger yet affordable property. He discovered a house at 54a Lower Circular Road, which was owned by a Muslim man who was going to live in Pakistan. At this time, there were still violent clashes between Hindus and Muslims and he felt vulnerable in an area that had such a large Hindu population. Archbishop Perier authorized a sum of money to purchase this property on behalf of Mother Teresa's order, but unfortunately the land alone was worth more than they could afford.

The story is told of the "miraculous" acceptance of the archbishop's offer: the Muslim went into a nearby mosque to pray and came out saying, "I got the house from God, I give it back to him." This may simply have been the case of a refugee accepting that this was the best offer he would get for a run-down building in what had become an unfashionable, even hostile area.

The Mother House

The house at 54a Lower Circular Road soon became the official headquarters of the Missionaries of Charity and was known as the Mother House. When Mother Teresa first saw the building, she thought it was much too large. "What will we do with all that?", she asked. Father Henry told her she would soon need the space and that the day would come when she would ask herself where she could put all the people she cared for. He was proved right, and over

▶ *As her order grew, Mother Teresa continued to provide hands-on care. Here she cares for a dying man.*

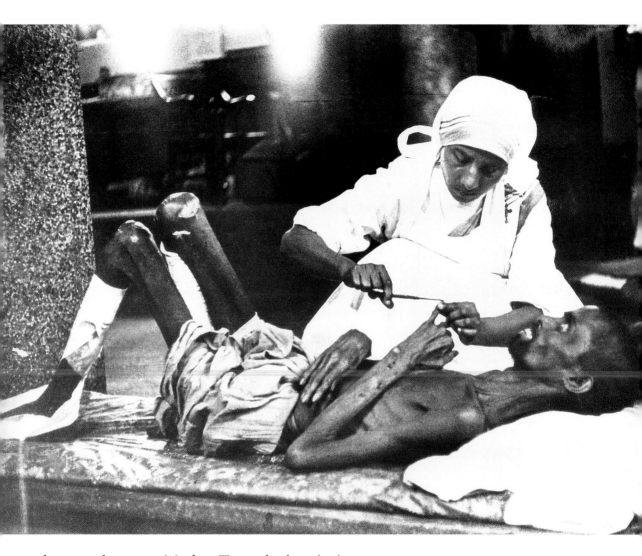

the next few years Mother Teresa had to search all over the city for further buildings in which to work and house her growing order and its expanding number of patients.

In the early 1950s there were an estimated six to eight million people

▲ *A sister attends to a dying man by cutting his fingernails and dressing his septic sores.*

living in Calcutta. Of these, 200,000 were living on the streets of the city, some of them dying on the pavements, alone and with no one to care for them. Mother Teresa once found a dying

No place for the dying

It was not unusual to see sick or emaciated men and women dying on the streets of Calcutta. Death in the Hindu culture is associated with pollution and impurity. Poor people on the point of death might be evicted from their living spaces and thrown onto the streets so that their rooms did not become "tainted". In the Hindu caste system, only the "untouchables" (the lowest caste) can handle the dead. Because of this, they are treated as outsiders and avoided by members of higher Hindu castes.

woman who was so ill that she could do nothing to help herself. Rats and ants were eating her feet while she lay in the gutter next to a hospital.

Mother Teresa lifted her in her arms and carried her into the hospital. She pleaded with hospital officials to let the woman have a bed in which to die peacefully. But hospitals in Calcutta were always full and would only take those who could afford to pay. They had no room for the poor masses, especially those who had an infectious disease and would need long-term care. In this poor woman's case, no hospital would take her in and she died on the

streets in spite of Mother Teresa's intervention. This sad event made Mother Teresa think about the need for a place where the terminally ill could spend their last days in dignity, tended with kindness and care.

Pure hearts

Mother Teresa was always aware of the importance of friends in high places. She had approached the Calcutta Corporation several times about improving the water supply to the slums.

The Calcutta Corporation health officer knew her and knew what a determined person she was. Mother Teresa also knew the chief minister of West Bengal, Dr Bidhran Chandra Roy. Roy had studied medicine in London and was the physician of both Gandhi and Nehru. He had twice been mayor of Calcutta in the 1930s.

The refuge

Mother Teresa went to the city hall to ask for help in finding a refuge for the dying poor. Maybe because of her previous dealings with these senior councillors, the corporation offered her the use of a run-down former pilgrim's hostel behind a temple devoted to the Indian goddess Kali.

As soon as she saw the old hostel, Mother Teresa accepted it. She knew that the nearby shrine attracted poor Hindus who were dying. The hostel, which was run down and filthy, was currently being used by a group of destitute people for drinking and gambling, but it had an ideal layout and both gas and electricity. It also had a large enclosed courtyard where washing could be hung out to dry.

The nearby temple of Kali, the Hindu goddess of death, was called the Kalighat. It stood in the centre of a busy main street and was a place where poor and destitute Hindus came to die. It was one of the most sacred places in the city for devout Hindus and these people were not happy when they discovered that a group of Christian nuns would be working almost next door to their shrine. They suspected that the nuns would use the site not only to help the dying, but also to convert them, in their last hours, to the Christian faith.

▶ *This photograph shows an area near the Kalighat in Calcutta.*

▲ *Dr Bidhran Chandra Roy, whose official efforts helped Mother Teresa in her work.*

Where there's a will, there's a way

Dr Roy, who was a respected politician in Calcutta, was one of many people who took notice of "the persistent little woman" in the white sari, who queued outside his office at 6 a.m. every day. Determination and persistence were an integral part of Mother Teresa's character. She knew what she must do to help those in need and she would not give up until her demands were met. Physically, she was tough. Even in her seventies, she was still walking the streets in search of destitute people to bring to her refuges. She was also practical. The unwanted children who were brought to her often needed round-the-clock care. Some were beyond help. For those who recovered and were capable of learning, some form of education or training was given. Older girls were taught to type and boys learned skills such as carpentry to improve their chances of getting a job when they left.

The Hindu priests (Brahmins) organized demonstrations against the use of the ex-hostel by Mother Teresa's order and regularly petitioned the city authorities to have the sisters evicted. However, nothing was done, and it was only when the Missionaries of Charity took in and cared for a young Brahmin priest who was dying with advanced tuberculosis that they were finally accepted by their neighbours.

Mother Teresa called her new establishment Nirmal Hriday, which translated from Bengali means "the place of the pure heart". On 22 August 1952, the feast day of the Immaculate Heart of Mary, the refuge was opened. The sisters needed a doctor in attendance at Nirmal Hriday and so they took on a young man who was still completing his studies at one of the large hospitals. He was 22-year-old Marcus Fernandes, a Catholic whose sister had been a pupil at Loreto.

A lack of care?

Not everyone who worked with Mother Teresa praised her methods. Some professionals found the basic level of care in her establishments frustrating. Dr Fernandes felt that the treatment of patients at Nirmal Hriday was neither efficient nor up to the standards required to make a correct diagnosis of their symptoms. Many who were thought to have tuberculosis, cancer or heart conditions were in fact suffering from extreme malnutrition. He suggested various methods by which treatment could be made more effective. He tried to persuade Mother Teresa to give the undernourished patients pulses and rice with added vitamin supplements to help them recover. But her stubborn streak was evident when she ignored his suggestion, leaving Dr Fernandes increasingly frustrated.

The doctor and his wife later went to London where he completed his postgraduate training at the London School of Hygiene and Tropical Medicine. When they returned, Mrs Fernandes worked on another of Mother Teresa's projects.

One of her tasks was to sort out medicines that had been donated from the USA. Most of these drugs were for western complaints, such as blood pressure, obesity, depression and other mental disorders. These were generally unwanted drugs from people's bathroom medicine cabinets and many of them were past their use-by date. Dr Fernandes explained to Mother Teresa that they urgently needed antibiotics and vitamins, but she didn't seem interested in the doctor's opinion and things continued as before.

Indian Catholics

In 1498 the Portuguese navigator Vasco da Gama rounded the Cape of Good Hope, leading the way for European expansion into India and other points east. Twelve years later, in 1510, his countryman Alfonso Albuquerque conquered Goa on the west coast of India and took command of Portuguese interests. His aim was to stay and so he encouraged mixed marriages. In 1542 Albuquerque was followed by the missionary Francis Xavier, who went as a representative of the King of Portugal and became one of the best-known Roman Catholic missionaries.

The missionary zeal of both of these men resulted in a thriving community of Roman Catholic Goans. Indians with Portuguese names – such as Michael Gomes and Marcus Fernandes – were Indian Catholics of Portuguese descent.

Even though Mother Teresa had some obvious failings, she was striving to take people off the streets and give them comfort and shelter, the first person to do so. Despite the criticism of some individuals, there was a great deal of goodwill towards the Missionaries of

▶ *A large part of Mother Teresa's mission was to care for abandoned and unwanted children. Here she cradles a young child in a Calcutta street.*

Charity, who were doing the work that should have been shouldered by a responsible government.

Shishu Bhavan

Mother Teresa had a special fondness for children and wanted to establish a

▲ *Love and concern is in evidence in the expression on Mother Teresa's face as she meets a baby in the slums of Calcutta.*

home for the large number of children who were abandoned in the slums every year. Before long she was told of another abandoned property, just a stone's throw from the Mother House. It had wide steps leading to the front door and a large courtyard, suitable for use as a play area. With the help of Dr Chandra Roy the Missionaries of Charity acquired the house and named it Shishu Bhavan, which means "the children's home". It was officially opened on 23 September 1955 and by 1958 there was enough space for 90 children to live there.

Soon, police and other city officials began sending orphaned and unwanted children to Shishu Bhavan. The children were fed and treated for illnesses and many grew well again. They even received an education at the home and, where possible, were put out for adoption with new parents in countries all over the world. Babies were only baptized if they were known to be Christian.

But there were tragic cases as well as success stories. Sometimes, whole families of children were abandoned or orphaned and some were found to be too ill or weak to survive.

To help Mother Teresa, the Indian government agreed to give her a grant of 33 rupees for each of the children in her care. Later, she decided to reject this offer because government rules insisted that she spend exactly 33 rupees on each child. She wanted to spend 17 rupees a head, but on more children, and wasn't about to compromise her principles.

The homeless of Sealdah Station

The vast Indian railway system was a legacy of the British Empire, but each large railway station became a refuge for the poor and homeless.

With partition and independence in 1947, masses of people travelled across the subcontinent, desperate to reach places of safety. Hindus and Sikhs headed away from their homes which were now in Muslim-dominated Pakistan. Muslims travelled to escape the religious hatred of the Hindus in India.

A station for a home

Sealdah Station is the Calcutta terminus for the Indian Eastern Railway. When the British left India, floods of Hindu refugees began to pour into the city via this station, fleeing from what was now the eastern half of Pakistan. Hungry and exhausted from their journeys, most of the refugees simply camped out where they had left the train. Many had abandoned their homes and belongings. Some owned only the clothes they stood up in.

The new refugees joined the estimated 4,000 people a day who had already arrived in the city in the years before independence. These were people from the countryside looking for a new life away from the unproductive soil of their fields and farms. Whenever there was a drought the number of these migrants increased, further stretching the city's ability to cope and adding to the population of the slums.

The Missionaries of Charity regularly visited the station terminus, where 10,000 people lived, ate, slept and died on the platforms and on the floors of the waiting rooms. Train passengers had to step over people who slept or crouched on the floor. The sisters handed out bulgur wheat and soya beans

▲ This photograph of an Indian railway station in the 1950s gives an idea of how many people congregated there. The train on the left has hundreds of people on its roof.

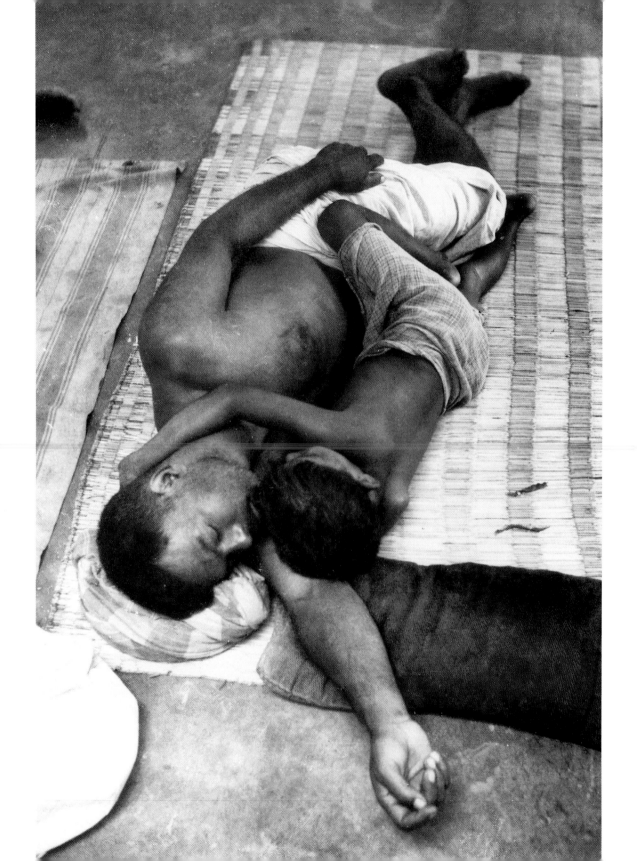

to those who had cooking facilities. They also set up vats to boil the grain and took round ladles of this mixture to sustain those who had no stoves.

Every day, those who were able and willing went into the city to try to find

Indian railways

- The British started building the railways in India in the mid-19th century.
- India has the fourth-largest rail network in the world.
- The longest rail journey takes 89 hours from north to south.
- There is more than 60,000 km (37,200 miles) of track.
- The railway system carries more than 10 million people a day or more than 3,650 million people a year.
- Most small towns and large villages are connected to the rail network.
- In 1950 more than 1.5 million people were employed on the railways.
- India has the most comprehensive railway network in the world, with direct trains linking stations more than 3,000 km (1,865 miles) apart.
- There are more than 7,000 railway stations in India

◀ *A scene in the slums of Calcutta. "Home" for this man and his son is a sleeping mat spread on a dirty station platform.*

work or at least something with which they could feed themselves and their families. Government officials came to select and take away fatherless families, who were then given shelter in refugee camps outside the city. Water was in short supply at the station since the only source was in the washrooms. Soon the whole terminus was littered with the debris of thousands of families, the air thick with the smell of smoke from cooking fires, human waste and rotting food.

The sisters came to the station as often as they could. They would scan the crowds for those most in need of help, particularly children who could be taken to Shishu Bhavan for medical attention.

Despite their efforts to remedy the situation, the numbers of refugees in Calcutta continued to grow. Since 1952 the population of the city has grown from about 8 million to an estimated 30 million people today.

The unwanted

Poor people who were hungry and homeless lived a dreadful existence, but it was much worse for those who had also contracted leprosy.

Lepers could find no refuge in Calcutta. Once there had been a leper hospital in the city but it had been closed down. A new hospital had been built well away from the densely populated city, but the poor, who relied on begging in the streets for their living, were not inclined to make such a journey.

Fear of leprosy

In the 1950s leprosy was still a disease which most people viewed with great fear. It was thought to be a shameful condition and the sufferers themselves often tried to hide their symptoms. Fathers who had become infected with the disease told Mother Teresa that they had had to leave their homes. If they stayed, their sons would not get jobs and their daughters would not find anyone to marry them. Such was the stigma attached to leprosy.

Mother Teresa decided to help the lepers in Calcutta and opened a shelter

A crippling illness

Leprosy still exists in some poor tropical countries of the world, largely in Asia, Africa, South America and the Middle East. Millions are affected. It is not a killer disease but a chronic, infectious illness, caused by bacteria. It destroys the body bit by bit, deforming and mutilating victims and also causing damage to the skin and nerves. One of the first symptoms can be a loss of touch. At the onset of the disease, light spots are usually visible on the skin's surface and these may develop into raised lumps.

If leprosy is not controlled, the disease can cause weakness, paralysis and the loss of fingers and toes. Because it is infectious and the symptoms are so unpleasant, lepers have usually been shunned or made to live in isolated groups known as leper colonies. Treatment with drugs is effective if the disease is detected early. Thanks to the efforts of doctors and volunteers, thousands of people have been cured of the disease in the last 20 years. Even so, poor countries often lack funds and personnel to administer treatment.

▶ *This photo of a leprosy victim demonstrates one of the disease's characteristic effects – loss of fingers.*

▲ Leprosy is still a problem in many areas of India. Here, lepers beg for food in the city of Varanasi, formerly Benares.

on the outskirts of the city at Gobra. This was only a small step, since the shelter housed just 150 of the estimated 30,000 lepers in Calcutta.

A few months later Mother Teresa set up a clinic at Shishu Bhavan. The clinic supplied 600 lepers with drugs that could help them control their disease. In addition to this, she set up a special street school for those children whose parents had the disease. The Missionaries of Charity taught the children at the school, keeping a watchful eye on them for early signs of the disease. Any child showing symptoms of leprosy could be treated while the disease was still in its infancy.

The mobile clinic

Before long the land on which the Gobra shelter stood was scheduled for building work and the leper refuge was closed down. Mother Teresa visited another possible site, but when she viewed it, a crowd drove her away with sticks and stones. They didn't want lepers living on their doorsteps.

Shortly after this Mother Teresa received a large donation from a Catholic relief organization in New York. This enabled the mission to buy a blue van and equip it with medicines, disinfectants and food. The vehicle was capable of carrying six people as well as its medical load.

On 27 September 1957 the Missionaries of Charity obtained a second van and Archbishop Perier proudly opened Mother Teresa's mobile leprosy clinic. The story was reported in the *Calcutta Statesman*, together with a photograph showing the archbishop and Mother Teresa beside the van. Once a week the van called at a number of centres in the slum areas of Dhappa, Howrah, Motijhil and Tiljala to hand out drugs for leprosy. Twelve months later the van was calling at as many as eight leprosy centres around the city.

In 1958 the Missionaries of Charity started working at an established leper community at Titagarh, on the northern outskirts of Calcutta. Mother Teresa had promised not to admit lepers to her home at Nirmal Hriday, so she brought the lepers who had come to her for help to Titagarh. An Indian rail company owned the land, a narrow stretch bordered by the railway line on one side and the sewerage works on the other. The company gave Mother Teresa the right to use this land so long as she didn't erect permanent shelters on it.

In the early days, there were several fatal accidents when trains collided with crippled people as they tried to cross the tracks. After two years the Titagarh municipal council offered Mother Teresa a piece of land on which she could establish a permanent settlement with a treatment clinic. Many

thousands of patients have since been treated there and large numbers have been cured.

A compassionate touch

In the 1960s a campaign was launched to raise funds and public awareness for leprosy sufferers. The campaign, run by Ann Blaikie, an English Catholic, employed the slogan "Touch the leper with your compassion". It was a great success and the money raised was used to set up a treatment centre at Titagarh

The Missionary Brothers

In March 1963 the Missionary Brothers of Charity – a new branch of the Missionaries of Charity – was given a blessing by the Archbishop of Calcutta. The original Brothers were a priest and 12 young boys, who lived on the first floor of the children's home, Shishu Bhavan. Their first task was to look after homeless boys who had drifted into the city and were scavenging at the rail termini of Sealdah and Howrah. Later, the Brothers became involved in caring for the lepers at the Titagarh refuge and, in 1975, they took over the running of the leprosy centre. Mother Teresa could not be the head

of the Missionary Brothers since the church does not allow a woman to take this role in a male order, but the two orders worked closely together. In 1966 an Australian priest, Father Andrew (Ian Travers-Ball) left the Jesuits to take charge of the Brothers. He had a more laid-back style than Mother Teresa and the two did not always see eye to eye. Changes brought in by Father Andrew included informal dress (the brothers wear jeans and shirts), a willingness to delegate, and more freedom of movement within the order. By 1990 the Brothers ran more than 90 homes in 30 countries.

▲ A photograph from the early 1960s showing a Missionaries of Charity van delivering medical supplies to Calcutta lepers. Visible at the rear of the vehicle is the "Touch the Leper" campaign slogan.

and a new leper community in the countryside outside Calcutta.

The Indian government then gave Mother Teresa a 30-acre site in the Asansol district about 320 km (200 miles) from Calcutta, where the mission built a community known as Shanti Nagar ("the place of peace"). Here, hundreds of leprosy sufferers were able to settle and live a relatively normal life in houses of their own.

Working refuges

Those living at the Titagarh and Shanti Nagar refuges today are partly self-sufficient. They make sandals and paper bags, which are sold to produce income for the settlements. They also weave sheets and make saris for the sisters of the Missionaries of Charity. Occupation centres, set up and run by the sisters, allow leprosy victims to work and earn a living.

◀ *A leprosy victim at one of Mother Teresa's refuges weaves a sari for the sisters.*

The making of a myth

In 1960 Mother Teresa took a trip outside India for the first time since she had arrived there in 1928.

She went to speak at a Catholic women's convention in Las Vegas in the USA. After the meeting she travelled around America, promoting her movement and making important contacts. She left New York, bound for Britain, Germany, Switzerland and then Rome, raising awareness of her mission and funds for it along the way.

In Rome she petitioned the pope to grant permission for her order to become a Society of Pontifical Right. Only after this application had been granted would the Missionaries of Charity be able to extend their work to other countries. In February 1965 Pope Paul VI gave his permission and the first mission was established in Cocorote, Venezuela in July that year. This was a great achievement for Mother Teresa, who always said that she never made plans but trusted in divine providence.

Hitting the headlines

Mother Teresa's work in the Calcutta slums had always received favourable notices in the Indian press. She became front-page news in 1962, however, when Bidhran Chandra Roy, chief minister of West Bengal, was interviewed on his 80th birthday. Instead of telling the reporter about himself or his colleagues in government, he preferred to speak about Mother Teresa. "As I climbed the steps of my building leading to my office, I was thinking of Mother Teresa, who has devoted her life to the service of the poor."

This report, and Mother Teresa's connections with other politicians and rich businessmen, mainly through

▶ *Pope Paul VI, who gave the Missionaries of Charity permission to expand into countries other than India in 1965.*

▲ Journalist and broadcaster Malcolm Muggeridge. His television programme Something Beautiful for God, aired in 1969, did much to popularize the work of Mother Teresa and the Missionaries of Charity.

their wives and daughters, led to her fame spreading abroad. In 1969 the British journalist Malcolm Muggeridge, who had lived in Calcutta in the 1930s, came with a BBC television crew to make a film about her work.

The "miracle"

Muggeridge was a devoutly religious man and a great admirer of Mother Teresa and her simple philosophy. He was so convinced of her special qualities that he claimed a miracle had happened during one of the filming sequences. As he told it, the technical crew experienced difficulties when filming in the house of the dying and didn't believe they had recorded the scenes. Some weeks later, when the rushes of the film were viewed, the darkened rooms of the refuge looked perfectly lit.

In fact, the chief cameraman had loaded a new type of fast film, which was designed for use in low-light conditions. No one at the BBC had tested this film before leaving Britain, but when the cameraman tried to explain the phenomenon, Muggeridge exclaimed: "It's divine light! It's Mother Teresa. You'll find that it's divine light, old boy."

The film was entitled *Something Beautiful for God*, taken from Muggeridge's interview with Mother Teresa, when she said: "Begin by making whatever you do something beautiful for God." Word of the "miracle" soon reached London journalists, who were quick to take up the story. Television and radio reports confirmed the miraculous circumstance of the filming and almost overnight Mother Teresa was being referred to as a living saint.

When Muggeridge's film was shown, Mother Teresa's fame spread around the world. A large number of people believed that this humble nun had changed their lives forever and donations began to pour in to the Missionaries of Charity. This was the beginning of Mother Teresa's new role as a public figure, one that would take her away from her home more and more. From this time onwards she spent much of her time travelling, making speeches and being seen with important people who supported her mission.

Pavement doctor

In 1979 an English doctor named Jack Preger, who had worked with the Brothers of Charity in Calcutta, set up a makeshift clinic for the poor, sick and needy under the city's Howrah Bridge. Unlike the Missionaries of Charity, Preger kept a card index of each patient, including their names and a simple address such as "under the bridge" or "the foot of the third lamppost". This was to give them some sense of identity. He was particularly concerned about the infectious disease tuberculosis.

Preger helped many destitute people in Calcutta, but unlike Mother Teresa he always fell foul of the authorities and his pavement clinic was opposed by the wealthy residents of nearby Middleton Row as well as by the city corporation. It took ten years, during which time Preger was frequently harassed and spent some time in prison, for his charity Calcutta Rescue to gain minimal recognition in Bengal.

In 1993 Preger was awarded an MBE for services to the poor and a special medal by the Royal College of Surgeons in Dublin, where he did his medical training.

◀ *Mother Teresa's deeply lined face was evidence of the hard work of caring for the poor and dying, but her wonderful smile also showed that such work held great rewards for her.*

True to herself

The press and media were responsible for creating the Mother Teresa myth. The woman herself, her beliefs and way of working did not change and she made no attempt to adapt to other people's expectations. She may have used the media, governments and the commercial world to fund her work abroad, but she made no value judgments about anyone so long as they enabled her to continue spreading her message.

Sticking steadfastly to her own creed, Mother Teresa was not swayed by good or bad publicity. She was only capable of doing things in her own way, which to many people seemed saintly indeed.

During their conversations, Muggeridge once said to her: "When I think of Calcutta and the appallingness of so much of it, it seems extraordinary that one person could just walk out and decide to tackle this thing." To which Mother Teresa replied simply: "It is He, not I".

Mother Teresa's way

From the start, Mother Teresa ran her order with an almost medieval austerity. All of her convictions about religious life had taken root by the time she founded her order.

Mother Teresa's traditional view of the Catholic religion infiltrated every aspect of her work and way of life. By the 1960s however, she was often at odds with the more informal ways of the church, which was trying to makes its doctrines more relevant to modern life. Many missionaries within the Catholic church were encouraged to dress more casually and be more flexible about times of prayer.

A strict rule

Life within Mother Teresa's order was strictly controlled. Personal possessions were kept to an absolute minimum, in keeping with the vows of poverty that all the sisters made on entering the Missionaries of Charity. Sisters were forbidden to accept personal gifts and were not allowed to receive personal mail. Their reading was restricted to books on religious subjects. Often they slept on bare floors or tables, with no cushions or blankets for extra comfort.

The sisters wore their distinctive white habits and organized their days according to a routine. The religious timetable imposed on the nuns meant that they worked during the morning between the hours of 8 a.m. and 12.30 p.m. At other times, Indian helpers took over in the refuges while the nuns rested, read and prayed.

Mother Teresa firmly believed that her sisters had no need to be aware of events in the world at large, at least in the early days of her mission. She assured them that they would learn

▲ *Life within – sisters of the Missionaries of Charity, clad in their saris, pray together. This picture gives an idea of the inside of one of their houses, with decorations and possessions kept to a minimum.*

Mother Teresa and the Catholic church

Mother Teresa's attitude to the church authorities was one of deference. She was not a rebel in any sense but worked within the rules laid down by the church. Consequently her work was sanctioned not only by her superiors in India but also by the head of the church in Rome. This was the main reason for her success in achieving what she had set out to do.

Her respect for authority and people in positions of power sometimes led her mistakenly to accept gifts of money from despotic political leaders. On her travels she made a point of reinforcing Catholic doctrines and was particularly vigorous in her condemnation of laws that supported abortion. She visited both the USA and Britain at times when debates were raging on abortion and lent considerable weight to the anti-abortion lobby in both countries.

all they needed to know from God. By putting their trust in the Holy Spirit, they would be guided through their tasks. Mother Teresa, who had trained as a teacher, felt that her helpers should not be better educated than the people they served, and she did not welcome nuns who had obtained university degrees. She believed that too much thinking "clouded and confused" the mind.

Help and support

It was to Mother Teresa's great credit that she inspired help and support from those with whom she came into contact. As word of her mission spread, huge donations flooded in from companies and corporations, western governments and large organizations worldwide.

Sometimes Mother Teresa was criticized for preserving the image of the Missionaries of Charity as an organization struggling to keep its head above water. Some said the Missionaries of Charity had enough money to build and staff several new hospitals in Calcutta, let alone bring their own facilities up to date. But this was not Mother Teresa's way. She preferred to extend her mission into other countries, helping as many needy people as possible, even if it

▶ *As the order grew, it acquired better equipment for its hospitals. This 1995 photograph shows a sister talking to an AIDS victim in Pnomh Penh, Cambodia.*

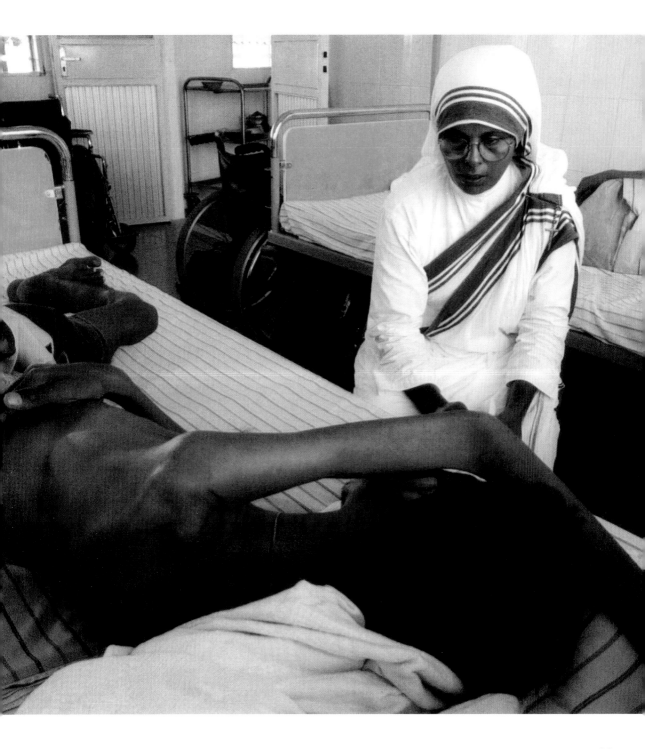

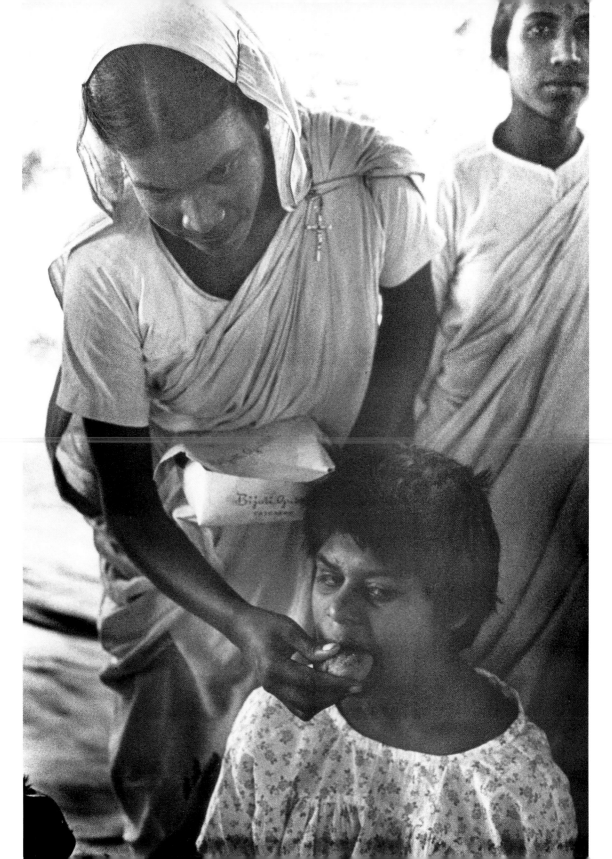

appeared that she was spreading the work of the Missionaries of Charity too thin on the ground.

Sometimes she may have taken her desire to preserve a pure and simple image too far. When a well-equipped refuge was donated in San Francisco, she gave orders for it to be stripped of all "luxuries" so that it would conform to her idea of how the nuns in her order should live. The benches were removed from the chapel, the carpets pulled up from the hallways and rooms and all the curtains were taken down. The comfortable mattresses and furniture that had come with the building were thrown out and during the winter the central heating was never used.

Single-mindedness

For nearly 50 years Mother Teresa stuck single-mindedly to her beliefs about how her order should be run. This may have been one of its strengths but she was criticized for her methods too. The sisters of the

◀ *Although some critics felt that, as the order grew, the personal touch diminished, one-to-one work went on. Here a sister helps to feed a handicapped child.*

The Poor Clares

Mother Teresa's insistence on a life of austerity outdid even that demanded of the Poor Clares, an order that was founded 800 years ago. Like the Missionaries of Charity, the Clares believe in a life of utter simplicity and that God's providence will supply them with all the things they need. But even the Poor Clares have access to newspapers, television and radio. The Clares also welcome university-educated nuns to their order.

Missionaries of Charity were never assigned to one task for long, making it hard for them to become competent at their job. They were given basic training in the care of the sick and dying, but sometimes they didn't know where they would be living the following week. This unplanned approach might have been exciting for a young girl, who had recently begun her vocation, but it could be frustrating for others who were more experienced and wanted some continuity in their work.

The Indian workers, who did most of the cooking, cleaning and menial jobs, were often over-stretched. They had few resources to deal with

the overwhelming numbers of sick and dying people who were brought to the Kalighat. As the mission grew, some volunteers who helped to wash and feed patients felt that the personal touch was missing.

As time went on, Mother Teresa was often away from Calcutta, caught up with the administration of her growing organization. Inevitably, she had less time to care for those in need, something she had never shied away from in the past. She had always been "hands on", looking after those in her care with love and compassion as well as doing her fair share of the everyday tasks.

The patients in her refuges were still kept clean and fed, but medical treatment was negligible. No doubt it was necessary for Mother Teresa to raise funds and greater awareness of her work, but she had come a long way from the early days of direct involvement with the poor and needy on the streets.

◀ *As time went on, Mother Teresa's commitments took her away from Calcutta more often. Here she is at London's Heathrow Airport on 24 April 1973 after flying to Britain for an awards ceremony.*

Mother of the world

Soon after Malcolm Muggeridge's television programme, Mother Teresa became a world-famous figure, an icon representing all the best aspects of Christianity.

In 1969, the same year that *Something Beautiful for God* was seen around the world, the International Association of Co-workers of Mother Teresa was recognized by the pope. This organization was instrumental in raising funds and setting up houses outside India in Mother Teresa's name.

A global message

Throughout the 1970s Mother Teresa received numerous awards from national governments and world organizations. New refuge centres were opened in all corners of the world, including one in Australia and another in Jordan in the Middle East. By the mid-1970s the Missionaries of Charity had founded more than 60 houses in India and 27 in other countries. It consisted of 1,133 sisters as well as many more co-workers and volunteers working to help the poor.

Mother Teresa's message was becoming known all over the world.

In December 1979 Mother Teresa was given the Nobel Prize for Peace and an accompanying cheque for $190,000. She received more than 500 telegrams from world leaders and was mobbed in the streets of Calcutta. The chief minister of

Awards and prizes

1971 Pope John XXIII Peace Prize
1971 Prize of the Good Samaritan, Boston
1971 Kennedy Prize
1972 Pandit Nehru Award for
     International Understanding
1972 Koruna Dut, Angel of Charity
1973 Templeton Prize
1974 Mater et Magistra
1975 Albert Schweitzer International Prize
1977 Doctor Honoris Causa in Theology,
     University of Cambridge
1979 Nobel Prize for Peace
1982 Doctor Honoris Causa, Catholic
     University, Brussels

▲ Pope John Paul II listens intently as Mother Teresa addresses more than 200 Catholic bishops at a synod *(meeting)* on 10 July 1980. Also listening is Archbishop Josef Tomko of Czechoslovakia.

▲ A great honour – Mother Teresa accepts the Nobel Prize for Peace in Oslo in December 1979. She gave the prize money, totalling $190,000, towards the work of her order, the Missionaries of Charity.

West Bengal held a reception in her honour and told her, "You have been the Mother of Bengal, now you are the Mother of the World."

At the ceremony in Norway, Mother Teresa modestly accepted the award with the words, "I am unworthy." She refused a further award of £3,000, which would have been spent on a banquet in her honour, asking that the money go to those who were in need of a meal.

By the early 1980s there were at least 20,000 co-workers in Britain alone and the organization, which had been developed by Ann Blaikie, had registered charity status. In little more than ten years Mother Teresa's co-worker network had become so successful that in the USA donations exceeded $1 million dollars a year.

When Ann Blaikie became seriously ill in the 1990s, Mother Teresa decided to close down the co-worker network. Her decision may have had something to do with the fact that the whole operation had become too large and too difficult to administrate, or that the Missionaries of Charity no longer needed to "spread the message". Whatever the reason, it ended in 1993.

In the 1990s Mother Teresa was becoming frail and her health was causing concern among her followers. By 1996 she was critically ill and spending most of her time either in a wheelchair or in bed. Elections for her successor were delayed as a result.

Finally, in March 1997, Sister Nirmala was chosen as the new leader of the order.

The wrong connections

Mother Teresa claimed she was not political, but sometimes she received financial and moral support from unexpected, even dubious quarters. One instance was the gift of more than a million dollars, which she received from Charles Keating, a businessman now infamous in the USA for his part in the Savings and Loan scandal of the 1980s. Keating was convicted in 1992 of stealing $252,000,000 from 17,000 small investors who had put their savings into his Lincoln Savings and Loan company.

At the time of his trial, Mother Teresa wrote a letter to the judge in which she praised Keating's character and charitable nature. After Keating's conviction, the deputy assistant attorney of Los Angeles County wrote to Mother Teresa explaining in detail Charles Keating's crimes and asking her to return his donation. He never received a reply or acknowledgment to his letter.

Back to her roots

In 1989 Mother Teresa made a private visit to Albania, the land of her forebears. She had tried to visit her mother and sister – who had moved to Albania from Skopje – 20 years earlier, before their deaths, but the Albanian government had refused her permission. This time she was able to visit relatives and friends and was granted her wish to set up two houses where her sisters could work among the poor. Within a year of her visit she had become a national hero in Albania, praised by both Christians and Muslims, and was featured on Albanian postage stamps and in its history books.

She was a 63-year-old Hindu convert to Christianity who had become a sister of the order in 1958. In 1965 she had been put in charge of Mother Teresa's first home outside India, in Venezuela.

On 5 September 1997, at about 9.30 p.m., Mother Teresa died of a heart attack at the age of 87. At the time of her death, she had set up nearly 600 homes in 130 countries all over the world.

Examining the myth

In the last few years of her life some parts of the myth surrounding the "saint of the streets" were closely examined. Over the years there had been revelations about the Missionaries of Charity receiving funding from dubious sources, as well as reports about the lack of medical treatment and secret baptism of the poor and dying in her refuges. In 1995 Mother Teresa received her first bad press in India.

The story, which concerned a married 15-year-old girl who had a child and was living on the streets, was reported in the *Calcutta Telegraph*. The girl had been badly burnt by fire and was admitted to hospital. After complaining about the treatment she was receiving, her relatives took her back to her familiar patch on the street. When her wounds became badly infected, one of Mother Teresa's volunteers told a reporter at the *Calcutta Telegraph* that the Missionaries of Charity would look after the girl. She was taken in one of their ambulances to each of their homes in the city. At the Kalighat she was turned away because she was not dying. At Shishu Bhavan she was refused entry on the grounds that she was not an orphan and was married with a child, although she herself was only a minor. Finally, she was turned away from Prem Dan because she was not insane or suffering from tuberculosis. This story caused much

▲ Sister Nirmala (left), who succeeded Mother Teresa as head of the Missionaries of Charity, gives food to a boy in Calcutta on Christmas Day 1999.

disillusionment in the city because Mother Teresa had always said that she never refused anyone.

A remarkable character

Mother Teresa's character had long been open to discussion. Some people commented on her need to be at the centre of events. And yet many of those who met her talked about how approachable she was and how important she could make a person feel, listening attentively as if you were the only person in the room who mattered. Her own view of her role on earth was: "I am like a little pencil in God's hand. He does the thinking. He does the writing. The pencil has only to be allowed to be used."

One thing is not in doubt: Mother Teresa was incredibly successful at what she did and was neither daunted nor squeamish about the task she set herself. Most of the criticisms levelled at her are about what she failed to do.

Some say she had a great opportunity to attack poverty and sickness at its source as well as raise the standard and quality of life of a great number of people. Perhaps, in her humility, she simply did not think about the vast amount of money she raised and how this wealth could be used to improve the condition of the people she served.

Certainly, one person could not save the world's poor and Mother Teresa was more interested in spiritual welfare than bodily welfare. Her simple message of love rested on her determination to save the souls of the poor and sick, and to comfort the dying and destitute. For a great many of the world's poor and unloved, she was their saviour.

▶ *Mother Teresa was given a state funeral on 13 September 1997. Here, her coffin is loaded on to a funeral gun carriage by the honour guard.*

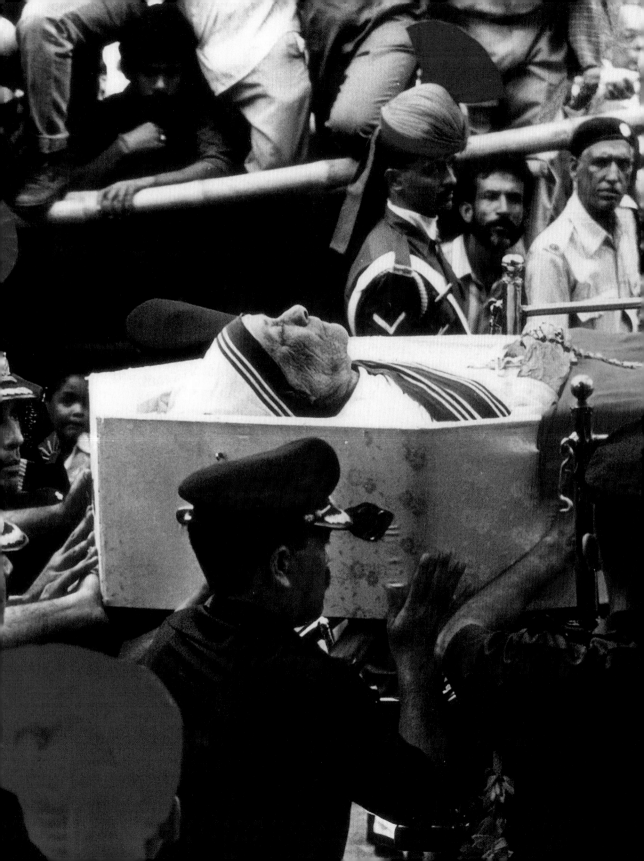

Glossary

adversity Position of bad luck.

austerity Harshness or strict moral code.

blight Frustrate or exert destructive influence.

British Raj British rule in India, from the Hindi word *raj* , meaning reign.

caste system Hindu hereditary class system; members of each caste are seen to be socially equal and have nothing to do with members of a lower caste.

compound Enclosure in which house or work building stands.

contagious A disease that can be passed from person to person by direct contact.

contemplation Thinking deeply about something.

debris Wreckage or scattered fragments.

delegate A representative sent to a conference.

devout Earnestly religious, with a strong sense of duty.

diocese A district under the spiritual care of a bishop.

diverse Varied, unlike something else.

equerry Officer attending a royal or noble person; traditionally an officer who looked after the horses.

evangelical According to the teaching of the Bible; preaching the Christian religion.

excerpt Passage from a book.

founder Someone who sets up an institution.

habit Dress worn by a religious order.

Hindu Someone who follows Hinduism, an Indian religion with many gods.

holy orders Sacred office of the Christian religion, entered into by someone who wants to devote their life to God.

hovel Small, run-down dwelling.

infectious A disease that can easily be transmitted from person to person.

Jesuit A member of a Christian order formed in 1534 to undertake missionary work.

malaria An infectious disease with chills and fevers, caused by mosquito bites.

minority Smaller part or number of people; a small group who differ from others in terms of race, religion, language or views.

Muslim Believer in Islam, a religion whose god is Allah and whose prophet is Muhammad.

nationalist Someone with patriotic feelings who believes in the independence of their nation and is prepared to fight for it.

novice Nun serving probationary period in a religious house, before taking vows.

noviciate Probationary period for novice.

nun Female member of a religious order.

nutritionist Someone who studies ways in which humans get nourishment from food.

obstetrics Branch of medicine and surgery relating to childbirth.

ordain To grant a priest holy orders.

Parsee Descendants of the Persians who fled Muslim persecution in the 7th and 8th centuries and went to India.

penance An action designed to seek forgiveness for a sin.

pilgrimage Journey made as an act of religious devotion.

prestigious Having a good reputation and influence.

province Principal administrative division of a country; district under supervision of an archbishop.

refuge A place of shelter from trouble or danger.

renounce Agree to give up or surrender a position or principle.

rosary Form of devotion in which prayers are repeated while keeping count of the prayers on beads.

scavenge Sift through what is not wanted or is thrown out by others.

secular About wordly matters, rather than spiritual ones.

Sikh Member of an Indian group, founded in the 16th century; Sikhs worship one god.

smallpox An acute, highly contagious viral disease.

sovereignty Possessing utmost power or control.

squalor Dirty, miserable state.

strife Struggle between opposing people or countries.

subcontinent Large landmass such as India that is smaller than a continent, but is geographically or politically independent.

turbulent Disturbed, riotous, unpredictable.

vocation Divine call or sense of fitness for an occupation or career.

vow Solemn promise to a god or saint.

whooping cough An acute infectious disease of the lungs.

Further reading

Chronicle of the 20th Century,
Chronicle Longman, London 1988

Mother Teresa
Navin Chawla
Sinclair-Stevenson, London 1992

Mother Teresa: Love Stays
Christian Feldman
The Crossroad Publishing
Company, New York and London
1998

Life Stories: Mother Teresa
Wayne Jackman
Wayland, Hove 1993

We Do It For Jesus
Edward Le Joly
Oxford India Paperbacks, Oxford and
New York 1998

Something Beautiful for God
Malcolm Muggeridge
Collins, London 1971

Mother Teresa: Beyond the Image
Anne Sebba
Weidenfeld and Nicolson, London
1997

*Mother Teresa: An Authorized
Biography*
Kathryn Spink
Harper Collins, London 1997

Lifetimes: Mother Teresa
Richard Tames
Franklin Watts, London and New
York 1998

Mother Teresa: A Simple Path
Lucinda Vardley
Rider Books, London 1995

Timeline

1910 26 August: Agnes Gonxha Bojaxhiu born in Skopje.

1912 Skopje becomes part of Serbia.

1928 15 September: Agnes leaves Skopje to join the Sisters of Loreto in Ireland.
1 December: Sister Teresa (Agnes) sails for India.

1929 Sister Teresa becomes a novice nun and starts teaching in Darjeeling.

1931 24 May: Sister Teresa takes her first vows and is sent to the Entally district of Calcutta to teach history and geography at St Mary's school.

1937 14 May: Sister Teresa takes her final vows and becomes principal of St Mary's school.

1946 16 August: Riots in Calcutta; Sister Teresa goes to find food.
10 September: On her way to Darjeeling, Sister Teresa has 'a call within a call' from God and asks for permission to leave the convent.

1947 Indian independence; riots in Calcutta and throughout the country.

1948 16 August: Sister Teresa leaves the convent to begin her work among the poor of Calcutta.

1949 19 March: Sister Agnes joins Sister Teresa as her first sister.

1950 Pope Pius XII approves the founding of the Missionaries of Charity.

7 October: Sister Teresa becomes Mother Teresa.

1952 22 August: Nirmal Hriday, the home for the dying, is opened.

1953 The Missionaries of Charity move into 54a Lower Circular Road (the Mother House); the first sisters make their vows.

1955 23 September: Shishu Bhavan, the first children's home is opened.

1960 Permanent refuge for leprosy sufferers opens at Titagarh.

1960 Mother Teresa visits the USA, London, Rome and Germany.

1963 March: Missionary Brothers of Charity start work

1965 February: Pope Paul VI allows the Missionaries of Charity to open refuges outside India; the first is in Venezuela.

1968 Refuges opened in Rome and Tabora in Tanzania.

1969 Mother Teresa opens Shanti Nagar for leprosy sufferers.

1971 6 January: Mother Teresa is awarded Pope John XXIII Peace Prize.

16 October: Mother Teresa receives John F. Kennedy International Award.

1973 Mother Teresa's sister Age dies in Albania, at the age of 70.

1975 Mother Teresa is awarded the Albert Schweitzer International Prize; the Missionaries of Charity now have more than 60 houses in India, 27 overseas, and 1,133 sisters.

1976 Indira Gandhi confers on Mother Teresa the Deshikottama of Doctorate of Literature of the Viswa Bharati University.

1979 December: Mother Teresa receives the Nobel Prize for Peace.

1983 Mother Teresa awarded the Order of Merit by Queen Elizabeth II.

1985 Mother Teresa goes to Ethiopia, where there is famine.

1988 Mother Teresa visits London to view the problem of homelessness; she meets Prime Minister Margaret Thatcher, hoping to gain her support in changing British abortion laws.

1988 The Missionaries of Charity now have 190 refuges in India and 225 overseas in 72 countries.

1989 Mother Teresa makes a private visit to Albania.

1990 Yasser Arafat, chairman of the Palestine Liberation Organization presents Mother Teresa with a cheque for $50,000 in Jerusalem.

1993 On a second visit to Albania, Mother Teresa is met and embraced by Pope John Paul II.

1997 5 September: Mother Teresa dies at the age of 87.

Index

References shown in italic are pictures or maps.

A

Albania 8, 10, 11, 98, 108
Andrew, Father 76

B

Bojaxhiu, Age (sister) 6, 9, 10, *10*, 11, 14, 98, 108
Agnes 6, 7, 8, 9, 10, 11, 13, 14, 15, 16, 106 *see also* Teresa, Sister
Drana (mother) 6, 8, 9, 10, 11, 14, 98
Lazar (brother) 6, 9, 10, *10*, 11, 13
Nikola (father) 6, 8, 9, 11
Bose, Subhas Chandras 33
BBC 83
British East India Company 28
British Empire 24, 28, 29, 68

C

Calcutta 4, 14, 15, 18, 22, 23, 28, 30, 33, 34, 38, 39, 40, 55, 56, 58, 59, 60, 63, 72, 75, 79, 83, 85, 88, 93, 99, 106
description of 24-25
slums of 26, 38, 39, 40, 42-47, 50, 66, 68, 71, 75, 80
Catholic Missions 18
Clive, Robert 28

D

Darjeeling 18, 20, 21, 24, 27, 38, 106
Doig, Desmond 51

F

Fernandes, Dr Marcus 63, 64
French East India Company 28

G

Gandhi, Mohandas 24, 30, *32*, 60
Salt March 32, 33
Gobra refuge 75
Gomes, Michael 45, 48, 49, *49*, 64

H

Henry, Father Julian 38, 42, 56

I

India 4, 11, 14, 16, 17, 18, 24, 27, 51, 94, 98, 102, 106, 108
before independence 28-34
partition of 34-37. 68
Indian National Congress 28, 30, 34, 37
International Association of Co-workers of Mother Teresa 94-97

J

John Paul II, Pope 95, 109

K

Kalighat 60, 93, 98

L

lepers 24, 72-79
refuges for *see* Gobra

and Titagarh
mobile clinic 75, 77

M

Medical Mission Sisters 39, 40

missionaries 4, 11, 18, 27, 86

Missionary Brothers of Charity 76, 85, 107

Missionaries of Charity 54, 56, 63, 64, 67, 75, 77, 79, 80, 82, 83, 85, 94, 96, 97, 98, 99, 107, 108

  expansion around the world 80, 94

  life in the order 86-91

  new leader of 97

  work with refugees 68-71

Mother House 56, 67, 107

Muggeridge, Malcolm 82, 83, 85, 94

  Something Beautiful for God 82, 83, 94,

N

Nehru, Jerwaharlal 37, 60

Nirmal Hriday 63, 75, 107

Nirmala, Sister 97, 98, 99

O

Order of the Poor Clares 14, 91

Order of the Sisters of Loreto 14, 27, 38

Ottoman Empire 6, 8

P

Paul VI, Pope 80, *81*, 107

Perior, Archbishop 38, 39, 47, 54, 56, 75

Pius XI, Pope 13

Pius XII, Pope 54, 107

Preger, Jack 85

  Calcutta Rescue 85

R

Roman Catholic Church 6, 13, 14, 21, 86

Roy, Dr Bidhran Chandra 60, *62*, 63, 67, 80

S

Saint Thérèse of Lisieux 16

Sealdah, station 68, 76

Serbia 6, 7, 8, 9, 106

Shanti Nagar 79, 107

Shishu Bhavan 66, 67, 71, 75, 76, 98, 107

Sisters of Loreto 14, 106

Skopje 6, 7, 8, 9, 10, 11, 16, 26, 27, 98, 106

T

Teresa, Sister/Mother

  awards 94

  becomes Sister Teresa 16

  becomes Mother Teresa 54

  criticism of 63-64, 98-100

  early life 6-11

  founds Missionaries of Charity 54

  fund-raising trips 80

  goes to India 16-18

  ill-health 97

  joins Order of the Sisters of Loreto 14-21

  learns nursing skills 39-40

  leaves Order of Loreto 39

  Nobel Peace Prize 94, 96, 108

  religious calling 11-13,

38, 106
takes Indian citizenship
54
teacher 22-38
work with children 64-67
work with lepers 72-79
Titagarh refuge 75, 76, 79, 107

V
Van Exem, Father Celeste
38, 45, 47
Victoria, Queen 28

W
Ward, Mary 14
World War One 9
World War Two 24, 33, 51